Prais

'Brave, raw and repeatedly sh...
breaks new ground for sports writing in Australia. It feels...
we have been waiting a long time for such openness from the
inside of professional sport. Like Andre Agassi's *Open*, this is
a transformative book; it is going to change our way of seeing.'
—**Malcolm Knox, journalist and author of *Bluebird***

'I was fascinated and shocked by the stories in this memoir,
but what really surprised and thrilled me was Jack's fearlessness as a writer, and his compelling voice. It takes so much
skill and diligence to make storytelling seem this effortless.
It requires courage to take such risks. Brandon Jack has talent
and daring in abundance.'
—**Christos Tsiolkas, author of *The Slap***

'Brandon Jack is a force for good. The kind of writer you want
every young man—wait, no, every man—to discover and read.'
—**Michelle Andrews and Zara McDonald,
hosts of the Shameless podcast**

'Brandon Jack is a great writer and this is a searingly honest,
unflinching account of a common side of sporting life that we
nevertheless rarely get to see. It tells the real story about the
guts and pain it takes to play sport for a living and the even
greater courage it takes to carve your own path to be the kind
of man you truly want to be.'
—**Peter FitzSimons, journalist and author of *Breaker Morant***

'Brandon Jack has turned a deeply reflective and unflinching
aesthete's eye within to write a startlingly candid, moving and
elegant memoir about masculinity, family, the compulsion to
win—and living with yourself when you don't.'
—**Paul Daley, journalist and author of *Beersheba***

28

BRANDON JACK

28

ALLEN&UNWIN
SYDNEY·MELBOURNE·AUCKLAND·LONDON

First published in 2021

Allen & Unwin
83 Alexander Street
Crows Nest NSW 2065
Australia
Phone: (61 2) 8425 0100
Email: info@allenandunwin.com
Web: www.allenandunwin.com

A catalogue record for this book is available from the National Library of Australia

ISBN 978 1 76087 677 7

Set in 11.5/17.5 pt Sabon LT by Midland Typesetters, Australia
Printed in Australia by McPherson's Printing Group

10 9 8 7 6 5 4 3 2 1

For blurred edges and Grace

'Of ugliness—To me there is just as much in it as there is in beauty . . .'

Walt Whitman, 'Thoughts' in *Leaves of Grass*

Contents

Author's note

After signing my first publishing deal, I locked myself away and spent every waking moment writing a manuscript. Then, upon submission, I was overcome by an inescapable emptiness—a dread that did not befit the amount of work I had just done.

For months the feeling persisted, and gradually I accepted that this was merely the reality of being a writer.

Then, while preparing to move apartments, I came across my old football diaries at the bottom of a taped-up cardboard box, tucked away in the back corner of my garage.

In my initial manuscript I had made it clear that I did not want to talk about football. I summarised my lifelong relationship with the games I had played to a series of dot points no longer than half a page. I had also made the request to my publisher that we keep references and images of my footballing past away from the promotion of the book. But re-reading the diaries from my years spent as a professional footballer, I saw something I had tried to escape. In the months that followed, I started writing again, and this book is what poured out of me.

As you read, please know that I do not intend this to be a direct comment on the games I have played nor the organisations

I have represented—both of which bring happiness to many people and which cannot be defined by a single perspective. Rather, see this is an attempt to understand my relationship with football.

Writing this book has been a significant step for me—I've achieved clarity I was unsure I would ever find.

So, persevere. There is joy. I promise.

Prologue

GUTTER

I'm standing in a gutter, stomping down on a premiership cup with the flat block heel of my scuffed black boot. I'm using my right foot out of spite—my sadistic way of saying that I don't need the left, the one that I spent all those hours trying to perfect.

Momentum, alignment, follow-through.

Don't bend your arm like that.

Don't jump when you kick.

Don't turn your hip.

Laces towards the target.

Fingers along the seams.

Cars driving past swerve to avoid me like I'm some sort of rabid dog foaming from the mouth. My teammates watch on from the entrance of Bar Cleveland in Sydney's Surry Hills, unsure whether to laugh or pull me away.

It's the very early hours of a Sunday morning. Bouncing off my chest is a medal engraved with *AFL Sydney Premier Division Premiers 2019* as the forcibly malleable metal of the cup my team has just won caves under the force of my boot: *Crack. Crack. Crack.*

This is what we play for, is it? Crack. Crack. Crack.

I won't be satisfied until it's smashed, broken, unrecognisably snapped in half.

Crack. Crack. Crack.

Come on you fucker. Break.

The road below is a dead treadmill upon which tin flashes of colour float. People yell at me, but their words are dulled as though hands are covering their mouths—my hearing is fucked from the six months I've spent between a crash cymbal and an electric guitar amp in an underground storage locker soundproofed by thin canvas. Still, I can hear my name being called: 'BJ, come on, don't! BJ . . .'

BJ. BJ is my football name. Hearing it perks my ears up and invokes a readiness from the cells of my body. It cuts through and makes *Brandon* feels foreign. Who even calls me Brandon?

'Yeah yeah yeah BJ BJ BJ!' a teammate would yell, their palms facing outward as they called for the ball. Then, from behind, the next in line cries, 'Got your back here BJ!' Sometimes I think that this BJ and me are separate people. He's the ego, the projection, and I've mostly just let him take over because it's less effort. But I don't know if that's true. I really don't know. That feels like the easy way out.

The final siren of the Grand Final sounded hours ago. We sang the club song twice—once on the ground, once in the sheds. I knew the first line but after that I had to look around, my mouth opening and closing to match the cadence of the verse and chorus for the rest of the song. I avoided eye contact so that no one noticed what I was doing.

The rooms then emptied and we sat on the ground in a circle with the score still on the board, lighting up the night sky, and drank. Then we piled onto the bus where there were more drinks waiting in an esky on the front seat. I grabbed a bottle of wine, which I finished by the time we arrived at the bar. I've been ordering double-shot vodkas since, snatching the ice out of the glass each time, throwing the cubes on the ground, and sculling the residual liquid in two gulps.

In between drinks I've been stumbling to the bathroom to do lines of coke off the top of the cistern through a tightly rolled twenty-dollar note. I don't like doing coke. I don't relish in it or glorify it. It's ugly. It's mostly always just a quick form of therapy: it makes me feel numb for a few minutes. But I can never fully enjoy those few minutes because though I am numb I can also see how soon they will end. With the note pressed inside my nostril I start counting down because I know that this night ends like all others have of late: with me on my mattress on my bedroom floor, a rickety pedestal fan looming over me as I stare at the ceiling, grinding my teeth, at war with the thoughts that fight to be the loudest. I hate feeling like I'm not in control. It's like a shadow that follows me, one that I first started noticing towards the end of my footy career. I would sit in team meetings and have to bite down onto the collar of my shirt because I was scared that I would scream something out. Then after training I would drive through the Sydney Harbour Tunnel to my band's rehearsal space, worried that my hands would violently jerk and veer me into the barricades on the side of the road. I would slow right down to forty kilometres per hour, my vision would get darker and darker like the edges of a black frame closing in, and I could feel my sweat on the wheel. Even in my dreams this shadow follows me: the car I'm in fishtails violently, side to side, but each correction I make pushes the rear bumper further from the centre of the road.

The black pants I wear have a hole in them from a dropped cigarette. The edges of the hole are orange and brown; through it, you can see my skin. It's been two years since I stopped playing professional football for the Sydney Swans. The room where I told them I was done is a few hundred metres away from the gutter I am standing in. I bought the boots I'm wearing now that same day, after I left for the final time.

I was twenty-three then, I'm twenty-five now. People ask if I miss it, and I say that I don't.

'Nah,' I say. 'I always wanted to do something else.'

If you tell a lie for long enough you can believe it, I guess. I just don't know which story is the lie.

Crack. Crack. Crack. Inward folded steel, disfigured and grotesque.

Thoughts enter my head.

A thought about money and how I only played football this year so I could earn a few thousand dollars to pay my rent.

That's the only reason I played this year, right? For money. Because I hate football. Football is a joke. A stupid game that I don't care about. Have never cared about. Will never care about. That's true, right?

Fuck, I don't even know anymore. I hate myself in this moment.

Our physio Viv steps off the footpath and into the gutter, putting her arm on my shoulder in an attempt to console me. 'BJ, come on,' she says. 'Come on, stop that.'

I shrug her off. She doesn't get it.

I grip the pole of a traffic light for balance and raise my heel once more, then drive my knee down like a piston. My teammates are still looking on. Uncertainty turns to shock. Their muffled voices move closer.

'BJ, come on, don't . . .'

'BJ. BJ! BJ . . .'

One of them walks up and stands before me, tall, thin, with just the hint of a sad smile on his face. He looks down at the cup we've won together, then looks back up and meets my eyes. 'Mate,' he says, slowly shaking his head. 'Who hurt you?'

I raise my heel once more and think about how I'll see the sun in a few hours and feel the whiplash from the night that's just been. I'm always thinking about tomorrow. Always thinking about tomorrow, because of yesterday. Never thinking of today. Never today.

Crack. Crack. Crack.

PART I

BUTTERFLIES AND
CHEWED-OFF FINGERNAILS

The first thing you'd see when you walked into the house I grew up in was a framed 1986 Australian Kangaroos rugby league jersey hanging on the wall. On a gold plate underneath it were all the scores from the Unbeatables tour of Great Britain and France: Australia 46, Hull 10. Australia 40, Leeds 0. Australia 38, Great Britain 16. Adjacent was a New South Wales Blues jersey with a photo of Dad underneath scoring his lone State of Origin try. In the room to the right were three Dally M Fullback of the Year awards and a black velvet box with a Golden Boot inside. The Golden Boot was given to the person judged to be the best rugby league player in the world each year. In 1987, this was Dad. He was only twenty-six years old. As a kid I would take it out of the box and hold it in my hands. It was heavy. For a long time I thought it was real gold.

In our kitchen was a boombox radio with a steel antenna that only caught frequencies when pointed in certain directions. We always ate at a table, though very rarely all at the same time because usually someone would have training and someone would be picking them up. Mum would put Glad Wrap over their meals and leave them on the bench so they could come home and put their plates straight in the micro-wave. Steam would rise again from the mashed potatoes, peas and whatever meat we ate that night.

Through the kitchen window you could see the entire backyard, closed in at the back by a rickety wooden fence constructed from broken palings that we would pull off the nails with surgical precision so we could squeeze through and retrieve half-taped tennis balls from our neighbours' yard. None of us were cricketers; we didn't have the patience for that game. We'd hold our breaths when a half-volley was scooped up in the direction of a window by the Puma bat we shared. During winter, the bat would be left face-down in the rain. The handle was wrapped in loose thread and the edges held together by gaffer tape.

We had a basketball hoop weighed down by a base filled with water. The net was tattered and beaten by the seasons— drenched in winter, scorched in summer. I think Mum had hoped that one of us would show an interest in one of the sports she had played. When I took up softball for my primary school, I remember she took me out onto our front lawn and taught me how to pitch.

We had a peanut-shaped pool, and a spa that in winter became a green bog with a frog living inside the filter box, and a backyard where I would kick a footy to myself, high up into the air so that it would fall back down through the clothes on the Hills Hoist which stood in the middle of the yard.

Our heights were regularly marked on the wall above the garbage bin in the pantry, and on our fridge was a photo of Kieren, Rhys and me wearing heavy cotton long-sleeved jerseys and football shorts, facing away from the camera with our arms bent and our legs stretched as if we're running, like the pose held by the frozen men atop Dad's trophies. In the photo I'm looking up at my brothers to make sure I am doing the pose right. You can't see my face, but I can tell that I am smiling.

To the left of the framed jerseys in the entranceway was a stairwell that took you up to the third floor, where all our bedrooms were. My parents' room was the second on the left; beside their bed was a large wooden chest with all of Dad's old jerseys inside it. The walls on either side of the stairwell were filled with team photos and action shots of my dad playing for the Balmain Tigers, New South Wales, Country and Australia. There would've been near fifty photos of him that I'd pass by dozens of times a day from the time I could walk until the day I moved out. Eventually more photos of Kieren and Rhys would join these photos of Dad—the first were of them turned at forty-five degrees, holding the point of a football towards the sky, smiling. That's how you look when you hold a football. Happy.

Of the lot, there was just a single photo of me. Aged six, with an opposition player wrapped around my ankles and a look of discomfort on my face as I tried to escape the tackle.

———

I guess it starts with rugby league in Manchester in the United Kingdom.

That's where my family moved in 1992 so that Dad could coach the Salford Red Devils. I was born two years later in the few months between the death of Kurt Cobain and the ascension of Oasis.

We lived in the town of Stockport, a town I know only through the grain of an old VHS camcorder, the tapes of which make everything seem forever familiarly distant: nostalgic and real, but always as the untouchable memory of yesterday. In the videos I have watched, our street looked eternally wet and cold and grey. All the houses were the same, with identical driveways, mailboxes, windows and doors.

The camera lens was mainly fixed on my elder brother Kieren, a manic flash of Man United red running wild, his blond hair cut in a perfect bowl. He gravitated towards football of any code, and action, always running or throwing or kicking.

In the wake of Kieren's chaotic energy was Rhys, his junior by two years, sporting the same hair cut in a darker shade— more like our mum's.

While Kieren gripped footballs and slid across the carpet, Rhys stood still, more observant of the world, sucking his thumb while the black beady eyes of a teddy bear in chequered overalls hung precariously by his side. Rhys was delicate and soft, with freckles on his cheeks. He had time and patience, both of which he used to draw pictures and construct things from plastic bricks.

Our Manchester backyard housed a soccer net into which my brothers would kick spherical footballs. Both were left-footed—Kieren more definitely so than Rhys. I always found that interesting because Dad kicked with his right, but then again Mum was left-handed, so I assume she'd kick with her left. We came back to Australia in 1995, the year after I was born, so that Dad could play football for the newly rebranded

Sydney Tigers. Five years passed, and then my memory begins. Mum and Dad are sitting me down on the bench outside my kindergarten classroom; having them both there gives the day a sense of importance. Dad holds my dangling foot in his hand and pushes the boot on. Size five, black laces, black studs, black leather and the Italian flag Lotto logo on the side. He puts the sole of my covered foot onto his knee, lifts the tongue of the boot and pulls the laces towards the sky. The pinky finger of his right hand sticks out at a forty-five degree angle, the lingering relic of an injury from returning the kick-off in extra time of the 1989 Grand Final that he has never had fixed. Or was that the finger that got caught in Steve Roach's training top? I get the stories confused sometimes. I think it's the latter. Anyway, I type these words with out-of-shape fingers of my own: arched pinkies on either hand, and a bulged knuckle on the ring finger of my left—the result of an unsuccessful attempt to catch a football a few years back.

Dad tugs my shoelaces with conviction, tying them into place. It's something he's done tens of thousands of times—on his own feet, on Kieren's feet, on Rhys' feet. And now my feet.

He presses his thumb between the top of my big toe and the end of the boot and asks me to move my toe up and down. There's about an inch of space.

'He'll grow into them,' Dad says.

That was one of the two things he always said about footy boots. The other was, 'They've got a bit of give, the leather will stretch.'

Dad tells me I should take a few steps to see how they feel. I stand from the bench tentatively; walking on studs for the first time is like taking to ice. It's not a natural feeling, studs on concrete. You need something to dig into—grass, dirt, sand, mud. I look ahead and run across the faded yellow markings of a hopscotch outline on the asphalt of West Pennant Hills Primary School.

'How do they feel?' they both ask in unison.

'Good,' I say, nodding my head.

The next thing I remember is playing my first game. My memory does that, blacking out between football events, or at least using the black as the marks to define the in-between.

I arrive at Greenway Oval in Cherrybrook on a cold Saturday morning, wearing padded black Steeden headgear. There is smoke from the barbecue floating in stasis above circular brick installations. Velcroed to my torso, concealed by the white-and-blue long-sleeve cotton top with the Penno Stags emblem embroidered on it, is a pair of shoulder pads which make me look like a cardboard box atop a pair of matchsticks.

I stand in line as the referees check our fingernail lengths and the sharpness of our studs. If your nails are too long or your studs too sharp you can't play.

A boy at the beginning of the line, Phillip of curled strawberry blond hair and chubby pink cheeks, who occasionally runs the wrong way with the ball, has to find his parents so he can get his too-long nails cut. When I look down at my outstretched fingers I can't be sure if my nails are too long, so I put my them in my mouth and start biting down.

The referee comes to me and I pull them out of my mouth. He gently presses the backs of his hands against the tips of my wet, chewed fingers before moving on to the next player. We take to the field and our coach Stu drags us by the jerseys into position so we can take turns running with the ball.

I've been moved to the receiving position, and coach Stu, with his hand on my back, makes sure I know which way I am running.

The ball, smaller than the full-size ones we have at home, falls into my hands and I hear voices from the sideline scream *GO, GO!*

I run straight at the people in front of me and am tackled hard to the ground. I stand, put my foot on the ball and roll it towards the player behind me who then passes it to the next player who does the same as me. This happens repeatedly until the final whistle is blown: a call for us to converge in the middle of the ground, shake hands and say 'good game' to one another.

After the game we walk to our car and Mum says something like, 'You should try running around people, so you can score tries.'

The following week we play the Hills Hawks. I look at the line of people in front of me and do as Mum had said. The first two times I put the ball on the paint of the try line and the referee tells me that if I do it again, then he won't award a try. He calls me Brandon and I find it weird that he knows my name when we've never met before.

The third time I cross the line I take a few extra steps past the white paint and plant the point of the ball into the ground. After each try the parents who crowd the sideline with their Styrofoam coffee cups in hand cheer and clap and my team-mates run up to me and pat me on the back. We then return to our half and get the ball from the kick-off.

After the game we huddle on the concrete under the tin roof of the changerooms and our coach hands me a trophy:

a small marble square base with a gold-spray-painted plastic man on top. Engraved on the metal plaque are the words 'Man of the Match'. My teammates—all without a trophy of their own—clap.

In the car ride home I cradle the trophy in my lap and sit making a wave with my hand in front of the cool air coming out of the air-conditioning vents in the passenger's side of Mum's maroon Mitsubishi Lancer. I still have my shoulder pads and my black Lotto boots on. There are swirls of dirt and grass stains on my knees.

Mum is on the phone to Dad, saying how well I played. She looks over to me and smiles.

I tell her that I'd had this weird feeling in my stomach before the game, as though there was a breeze inside me and my heart beat faster because of it. I don't have the words to describe it, but she knows what I am talking about.

'What is it?' I ask.

She looks at me again, then back at the road. 'Those are just butterflies, Brandon,' she says.

'Butterflies?'

'Yeah, butterflies. They mean you're excited.'

EVERYONE CALLED
HIM JIMMY JACK

I caught the bus home from primary school every afternoon. The number 7 bus route went past the Koala Park and turned right onto Edward Bennett Drive.

I always sat on my own on the bus, my bag on the seat next to me.

My arm would rest on the window ledge and I would stare down at the protruding bony lumps which formed at the base of my hand. I'd wrap my fingers around the wrist on the ledge and grip tight, and my thumb would reach between the second and third joints of my middle finger. I'd memorise where the tip of my thumb reached, and hope that next time it wouldn't be as far.

Midway around the bend after Curtis Close I would stand up and walk towards the front. I'd grip the railing next to the driver then look down to make sure my laces were still tied. I always wore black runners. Never Clarks school shoes.

'Just around the corner,' I'd say to the driver, thinking that he hadn't seen me. I was always worried he hadn't seen me.

The bus would slow to a stop, the hydraulics would lower us down and the door would open. Then I would fling myself out onto the footpath and start to run. The first few steps were manic. My backpack swung from side to side as my feet crossed the varied textures of Cherrybrook driveways. There was no form in my gait, just hellish intent for 70 metres until I reached the corner of our street, where I would duck my head and glance to my right to see where my opponent was. I always imagined everyone on the bus watched me run with their faces pressed against the glass.

The bus driver would beep his horn in recognition of our contest as he continued down the stretch of road. I'd walk up the hill, breathless, and smile to myself thinking that I was faster than the bus.

I liked sprinting. I liked the wind rushing against my face and the feeling of the ground being pulled beneath me. I was athletics champion most years at my school and did Little Athletics over the summers at Ern Holmes Oval. I stopped the year that the lead leg of our four-by-one relay team, Jordan, arrived late to the state carnival. 'I'll just run both legs, that's fair,' were my words to the person holding the clipboard under a blue gazebo.

'Sorry, that's not allowed,' was the response.

So my teammates and I just stood on the track when the gun blew. The lanes to our left and right ran past. I walked past Jordan on my way out of the stadium. He was smiling slightly apologetically, like it was no big deal.

We lived on a cul-de-sac that dog-legged to the left as you walked up.

One day Kieren had pissed Dad off, I'm not sure what about—I think he had hit Dad's car with a ball—so Dad took his footy and booted it over the house where old Bob lived with his wife and his dog who used to chase me home in the afternoons. The ball ran down into the front yard of a house on the other side of Edward Bennett Drive. It was a torpedo punt that spiralled perfectly through the air.

Our house was the dead centre of a street that never had any Christmas parties or communal gatherings.

There were other kids on the street, but we weren't friends. Four houses down on the opposite side of the road lived two boys who would walk their whippets every day. They were skinny and had long hair and I thought they were strange.

It was like in that neighbourhood we all tiptoed around each other. If a person walked past you, you didn't stop and say hello. Everyone just kept to themselves.

Across the road from our house was a gunmetal-grey light pole which I would pass or kick a footy at every afternoon. The pole narrowed at the height where a player's hands would be to catch the ideal pass. I would dart to the right then plant my foot hard and shift back to the left before rolling my hand over the ball so that it would move through the air in a dipped trajectory. The ball would hit the pole, then the road, and roll along the gutter.

Day by day, week by week, the grip on the footy would wear away till the surface was shiny and smooth.

That was the sign of a well-used football, and I always thought that footies felt better when they were smoothed down and were more round than pointed at the stitches. Other signs that a football was mine were that the tips were flaking from being bounced on the ground repeatedly, and the middle of each of the four panels that were stitched together had a dent in it from the footy being spun on my finger like a basketball.

To the right of the light pole was a long driveway which gradually inclined for about two hundred metres. It led to a specialised care home and the back of a school for children with hearing impairments. Every afternoon the residents would come down and collect their bins and walk back up. They had their daily rituals, I had mine, and often they coincided. I would sit on the lawn waiting for them to walk back up before commencing again.

The front yard was where games of football were played between me and my older brothers. The try lines at either end were where our neighbours' lawn started. Our property was the football field, and the left-hand flank was riddled with bindis.

The end I would always head towards had a large pine tree in the in-goal area and a series of sharp jagged rocks beside it. If the ball went dead in goal, I'd scramble under the pine branches to collect it. Our concrete driveway was neutral territory, meaning that if you had the ball you could cross without being tackled. As a result, tries were either length-of-the-field efforts or some sleight of hand orchestrated from a metre out.

We'd play most afternoons. I'd beg Kieren or Rhys to come out with me, then I'd lose, and I'd cry, but I'd always come back the next afternoon and beg to play again.

Our driveway sloped down into the garage. During summer I would stand on it barefoot and play tennis against the front of our house. The slope would make the ball bounce up nicely, making it easier to hit the gap between the bedroom windows and the rolled-down garage doors.

In the garage there was a rusted weight set with a maroon padded bench, and a chin-up bar screwed to the ceiling with a string of socks tied to it with a cricket ball in the end. Occasionally the garage would flood, and so we would place the blue steel plates on top of towels and bedsheets to stop the water entering the house. Our boots and runners were kept by the wooden door, piled on top of each other. This part of the house smelt of petrol and grass.

Hidden beneath a pile of boots and football bags in the garage was a framed photo of my father with a disfigured face. In it his eyes were swollen shut, with stitches below the left and above the right. The image was in black-and-white; in colour it might've been too grotesque, but even still you could tell that his eyes were purple.

In 1991 there was a fight in the game between Manly and Balmain. Dad threw a punch over the top of the pack, and his momentum carried him away from the main melee. A Manly player held Dad while Ian Roberts uppercut him repeatedly to the face. Growing up, I was told a different version of events: that Dad was held back by the arms at half-time while the rest of his team had walked off the field. This wasn't completely off the mark, but it wasn't completely true either.

In the time since, Roberts has said that his violent actions were fuelled by off-field circumstances and has apologised with heartfelt sincerity about the incident both publicly and in private to my father.

His softly spoken words in the interviews I've seen do not match up to his on-field persona as one of the game's most brutal enforcers. It's like a metamorphosis took place between the footpath and the field. Though Roberts—the first openly gay professional rugby league player—did once say that homophobic slurs from opponents and crowds were like *gasoline over the fire* of his on-field aggression.

I'm unsure why, but the photo of my dad with stitches in his face was framed, maybe because it was used as evidence in the ensuing court case, or maybe because he took pride in the marks—like they were battle scars that proved a point. Whatever the reason, I thought he looked tough, and I wanted scars like his on my face. I saw it as part of being not just a footballer, but a man.

———

One day one of my primary school teachers, Mr F, covered the back of the classroom in black and orange paper and said, 'I bet you like those colours, don't you?' I responded by laughing. Those colours, the colours of the Balmain Tigers, were the ones I would always use to colour in the clothes of people I drew.

In Year Two we had a class presentation where we had to dress up as what we wanted to be when we grew up. In the lead-up we had to tell our teacher Mr Sandercock our idea so he could help us figure out our costume. When I went up to him, he said, 'Let me guess . . .'

I wore an Australian Kangaroos jersey with number 1 and the name 'Jack' on the back. My classmate Ryan Henderson was narrating the dress-up reveals and said '. . . and I know I'll never be as good at footy as Brandon.'

On cue, I ran out onto the stage, threw a footy in the air, caught it on its way back down, and ran off the other side.

People would often stop our family on the street to talk to Dad, and because of this and other similar experiences I always felt that we were *special*. Special because of Dad's football career—even if for a while I had also thought that everyone else had a dad who had played fullback for Australia.

Everyone called him 'Jimmy Jack'. They'd tell me he was a tough bastard.

He had his front teeth knocked out on North Sydney Oval in 1988 when tackling Mark Coyne. Blood streaming from his mouth, he found his teeth on the ground, put them in his sock and played out the rest of the game.

I never saw him play—he retired the year after I was born. A lot of people tell me that the '88 and '89 Balmain Tigers were the unluckiest team in rugby league history. At the Royal Oak Hotel in Double Bay a man with grey hair and a few missing teeth told me that Benny Elias, Wayne Pearce, Jimmy Jack and Blocker Roach broke his heart. As a kid I would bring up '89 if I wanted to upset Dad. He'd usually reply with something like, 'Talk to me after you play 244 games.'

Older men always had a glint in their eye when they saw him. They wanted to stop and talk to him like they were old school-mates. 'So, what're you doing these days, Jimmy?' Or, 'Whadya you think about the Tigers this year?' Or, 'Ah, and what about fullbacks today, who reminds you of yourself . . . Mini?'

I'd hide behind Dad's leg, silent, staring up at the strangers. They'd look down at me and ask if I played rugby league. I'd smile and nod and they'd say, 'You end up half the player your old man was and you'll be alright.'

FISH HOOKS

'It's easy, you just gotta touch the dangly thing at the back of your throat.'

As the words left his mouth, Kenny made a hook with the index finger of his right hand and pushed it deep into the back of his throat. His chest caved forward towards the ground, his shoulder blades shot back and his head convulsed like a seismic wave rolling under heavy earth. His fingers flew out of his mouth and thick yellow liquid dribbled onto the grass between his bare feet.

Kenny's parents were both cops. His dad had a bald head, a beer gut which he usually concealed beneath a club polo, and a white handlebar moustache. His mum was regularly seen in front of cans of Coke and chocolate bars in the canteen at Crestwood Oval. He had two brothers like me, though he was the middle child. His youngest brother Sam received a similar treatment to me—him with lots of tears and lots of screams of *Get off me, get off me!*

Kenny had olive skin and a small white scar on his face. His eyes were ice blue and he had lemon-bleached blond hair which he pulled through the top of his grey Canterbury headgear. A lot of boys in our team wore Canterbury head-gears. It was one of the many things—larger field, football bags, playing in positions, a piece of paper with set plays on it—that made me feel like I was moving into a more serious part of the footballing world. I begged Mum to buy me one of the headgears, and she did, but it didn't sit on my head like Kenny's did, and the velcro chin strap was uncomfortable and would slide around, so I had to readjust it every time I was tackled. I only ever wore it for one game and then it found its resting place at the back of my wardrobe.

After four years with the Pennant Hills Stags, 2004 was my first year with the Hills Bulls, and it was the year I went on my first football camp. I'd followed Rhys' lead into the Paramatta competition, as playing in the Parramatta competition gave you more of a chance at playing Harold Matthews and SG Ball for Parramatta, who were always one of the best teams, alongside Penrith, and that gave you more of a chance to be recognised by scouts. There was a politics to football that was well-known in our house. The teams you played for, and the competitions they were in, were always under consideration, with choices geared towards the ultimate goal of playing pro-fessionally. A discussion was had about sending me to Patrician Brothers' College in Blacktown in Year Eight so that I would have a better chance to make the NSW Schoolboys teams. Dad knew the headmaster, or someone high up, but I found a way to dampen that conversation.

Dad had been on football camps. Kieren had been on football camps. Rhys had been on football camps. Now I was going on a football camp. My first football camp. Everything comes in firsts: I remember my first game. My first try. My first of anything with football. The first time I had my ankle taped I said to the physio: 'I feel like a real footballer now.' Even drinking my first sports drink—an orange Gatorade downed on the tenth fairway of the Forster Tuncurry Golf Club—is a vivid recollection.

———

We—the under-tens Hills Bulls—huddled in the backyard looking at Kenny's vomit on the ground. In every social circle there are codes: haircuts, clothing, patterns of speech; they are the norms, behaviours, attitudes and values that give one a sense of place. For us back then, forcing ourselves to throw up was our rite of passage. It didn't make sense—which meant it made all the more sense, because it was ours.

We each took turns manoeuvring our fingers into the backs of our throats. We'd bend over, face the ground, and retch from our mouths. The sound of our dry heaves and childish laughter echoed as heads jolted back and forth.

I put my fingers together, opened my mouth and made the hook. I reached for the little punching bag at the back of my throat, realising it was further away than I first thought. I pushed deeper until I felt like I was going to choke. But still nothing came out. Encouragement from teammates followed. 'You've got to really touch it.' 'Hold the fingers there till it comes out, don't stop till it does.'

I was the new kid. Most of these guys had played together since under-sixes, but I knew whenever I played footy that I would fit in because I could hold my own on the field and my teammates' dads would tell them who my dad was.

I pushed deeper, with my thumb now by my earlobe, my crooked index finger riding along the roof of my mouth.

Deeper, I thought. *Go deeper. Throw up, fucking throw up. Come on.*

I felt the smooth lump where my throat met the roof of my mouth expand to hold down the upcoming heat of bitter stomach acid. Water was leaking from my eyes. Then it happened. The yellow liquid came out, and a line of spit dangled from a thick clump on my lower lip. I whisked it away with my hook and the spit dangled from my finger till I wiped it on the grass.

Our coach Stoney walked down the wooden stairs. 'What are you blokes doing?' he said. He was a lumbering man with heavy feet that made the wood creak.

No one responded.

'Come on then, put your gear on, we've got training.'

We walked to the beach, passing a tackling bag between us. Stoney said that the bag wasn't allowed to touch the ground, and if it did then we'd have to each do fifty push-ups. I couldn't do fifty push-ups and started wondering how I could fake that I could.

The bag was a long, red, thick padded cylinder with black handles on the side. Foam padding spilled out of a slit in the place where shoulders would hit it time after time. It was the kind of tackling bag that fills the storerooms of every local rugby league club, the kind that when struck makes a sound like pressurised air being sucked out of an aeroplane cabin.

Our props Chris and Craig did the bulk of the carrying. Craig was the star child athlete. One of the best baseballers in the world for our age, and the best player in our comp for footy too. I ended up going through high school with Craig, and I watched Kieren's first AFL game from his living room. Craig stopped playing baseball midway through high school. He played First rugby for our school, but never ended up being what everyone thought he would be back then. He lives in Queensland now, and is engaged, and in the photos I've seen he looks happy.

Chris, on the other hand, seemed to get more pain from football than anything else. I could always hear his dad, who was much smaller than Chris, yelling out from the sidelines for him to go harder. Chris would take the ball and run in an unbroken straight line at the defenders in front of him. When he got worked up the pitch of his voice would rise, and his eyebrows would converge in the middle of his head. He was the kind of kid who wanted the others to like him or fear him. I once saw him almost cry on the field for giving away a penalty.

———

On the final night of the camp, Kenny, Jordan and I found a spot under a hanging rock which we thought would be good for a bonfire. We stood proudly over what we agreed was the perfect hollow until Kenny's older brother came by and said the spot was no good. We moved to the middle of the beach and started digging a hole so that the wind wouldn't stop the embers turning into a flame. I'd never made a fire before, but pretended I had by watching what the other boys did and replicating it a few seconds afterwards.

I ventured into the tree line behind the beach and grabbed handfuls of leaves and sticks. When I dumped them on the sand Kenny's brother said that we didn't want too much greenery because it'd make smoke. Instead he said I should back go for the brown stuff, the dry dead stuff. I went back in and ripped rotted branches from the trees.

'That's better,' he said when I returned.

The others from the camp joined us as the sun set for the 'talent show' we had arranged. The one rule was that making yourself vomit was not a talent.

The dads were all wielding beers. I'd never seen my dad as much of a drinker. He'd have a beer at dinner, but I'd never seen him drunk—never slurring his words or coming in the front door late at night. I couldn't really remember him ever going to the pub either.

There was never much alcohol in our house—just a few bottles of wine in a steel rack next to his trophies, which were never opened. But this night at footy camp I do remember my dad laughing a lot as he drank with the other dads. He seemed happy. Relaxed. Every so often he would push down on his nose where cartilage should have been but wasn't.

The talent show ended when our knock-kneed halfback ripped his clothes off and ran naked around the bonfire.

We threw sand on the last of the burning embers and walked back to the house. The dads grabbed a slab from the fridge in the granny flat where we were sleeping and took it up to the house. When they were gone we raided the fridge and grabbed a few beers for ourselves.

'Oi,' said one of my teammates. 'There's some girls down the road—should we go check them out?'

We stole more drinks, then walked on the beaten road taking turns drinking from VB stubbies. When the bottle came to me I wrapped my lips around the neck and took a sip. I'd never drunk alcohol before. It made my throat itch and pushed my cheeks towards my eyelids.

We could hear the girls and moved towards their voices. 'There? There. There!' we said in excitement.

There were four of them sitting on plastic patio furniture on the second-level veranda. Empty wine bottles lined the base of the flaking white picket railing.

One of the boys started yelling, 'Hey, can we suck on your tits!? Come on, let us suck on your tits.'

'Ha. Are there any older guys with you?'

'I'm old enough, come on, let me suck on your tits.'

The beer came back around and I pursed my lips together this time, pressing the opening against them, so that when I tipped it upwards the liquid hit my lips and bounced back into the bottle. 'Fuck that tastes good,' I said.

I could hear waves crashing in the background, and the moon was full overhead.

THE BOY ON THE WING

When I was eleven I played league with a boy. He played on the wing and I played at fullback. He had rosy blushed cheeks and a raspy voice. He was about my height, and of a similar frame, and we had the same sandy-blond hair. His face was much softer than mine; I've always held tension in my face. Well, not always—there is a photo of me in kindergarten smiling with my teeth fully exposed and the word that comes to mind when I look in my own eyes is *cheerful*. I've never seen another photo of myself like it. Even in the annual school portraits I stopped smiling and started smirking. A lot of people say I don't smile enough. I come across as rather melancholy and people think that I'm unfeeling or bored because of the sternly blank expression I wear, but that's just me.

The boy comes to my mind from time to time, always frozen at that age when we played league together. At training I would stare at the boy and whenever he ran with the ball I'd hope he wouldn't get tackled. I'd find myself cheering inside my head, willing him on to score a try.

My teammates said he had a violent streak, a form of ADHD, but I could never imagine him hurting anybody.

———

There's a specific Friday night that I remember because the Roosters were playing the Broncos and Darren Lockyer wore the number 6 and a young Karmichael Hunt was at fullback.

Hunt was the reining Dally M Rookie of the Year. He had debuted at seventeen years of age and had these thick tree-trunk legs that made the seven-year age gap between us seem wider than it ought to be. He also had a step like I'd never seen before. I wrote down on a blank page in the back of a Balmain Tigers autograph book how I thought he did it. *Jump. Move one leg in front of the other. Push off leg that comes down.* I practised it in the space behind the green velvet L-shaped lounge in the living room.

Friday night football was a ritual in our house. It meant that the weekend had arrived, and the weekend was sacro-sanct—for football. Monday to Friday were just days that passed so that the weekend could come around, and to me Friday was the best day because it was a space between school and football, a nothing time that I could float through unimpeded.

My family would sit glued to the black box. We spent most of our non-football family time either in front of the TV or at the local Italian restaurant in Cherrybrook owned by our family friends—though I use the term friends loosely, as we only ever saw one another at their restaurant—Nick and Liz, eating with Kieren's junior footy coach and his family who were our closest family friends. During the week our TV would display shows like *Cold Case*, *NCIS*, *Heroes*, *Lost* and *Prison Break*, but on Friday nights it was always football.

Every Friday there'd be a block of Cadbury chocolate and a bag of Pascall marshmallows placed on the coffee table, and I would sit directly in front of the gas heater so that my legs would press against the heated wire frame. Mum would warn me not to get too close. 'You'll catch on fire,' she'd say. I'd pretend to move and then slowly push my bare leg back on the frame.

Sometimes there would be an old bath towel—usually with a yellow-brown stain from sitting beneath rusted weights—laid out in my spot. Dad would grab a bottle of baby oil, and we would take turns lying down and he would give us boys leg massages. Other times there'd be wet football boots with their tongues stretched up and laces pulled out on top of a towel because they had to be dry by the following morning.

I'd move away from the heater to break off two squares of the chocolate, which I would shove in my mouth and suck like lozenges until they dissolved down to nothing. I'd seen my brother Rhys do this once, and from then on I took pride in being able to withhold the temptation to bite down. The block was never finished, so I'd sneak down on Saturday mornings before everyone else was up and quietly break off a row and start eating it while running back to bed.

At half-time while watching games at home, Dad would go and make Nescafé coffee or peppermint tea for Mum and Rhys, which he bought down the stairs on a plastic tray with an assortment of biscuits. I would always just have a glass of water.

I had a trial game in Newcastle one Saturday morning. On the car ride up I stared out the window, searching for a place to hide—a game I liked to play on long car trips. I'd pretend there was an alien invasion or a zombie apocalypse or a world war breaking out, and I'd try to find a place where I thought no one could ever find me. I'd look for somewhere unassuming, like a ditch twenty metres off the highway; I chose such places because they were almost stupid to hide within on account of how close they were to a place that was not hidden at all. The obvious spaces, the ones in the distance in the valleys and ridges, would be checked first, I thought. The best place had to be somewhere so menial—so barren, so nothing—that it was perfectly inconspicuous, and thus safe.

While I stared out the window on this trip, participating in this game that I had made, I was thinking about the boy in my team. I was thinking about how soft his face was, and then, for the first time while thinking about him, I thought about what it would be like to kiss him.

———

I remember this boy in my team being late to this game, and I was upset that he wasn't there. He arrived just before kick-off, said sorry to the coach, and we took to the field. From fullback I yelled at the defenders to slide left and right. 'Craig, left! left!' And 'Chris, right, right, right!'

At our first training session I had been asked what position I was. I'd never played a position before, but Dad was a fullback, so I said fullback.

Dad had told me that fullbacks were the eyes for the rest of the team, as from the back you could see the gaps that no one else could. I felt like I was doing the wrong thing if I wasn't constantly moving the players in front of me. I tried to have all the defenders exactly the same distance apart, creating an impenetrable brick wall from the bodies of eleven-year-old boys.

On the fifth tackle of each set I called the boy back from the front line. When I said his name he turned his head and ran back towards me. The opposition kicked the ball and it would land between us. One would return the ball, while the other would be the support.

After the game Dad drove Mum and I to a shopping centre for lunch. We had McDonald's from the food court. I had plastic chicken batter between my teeth which I swished around with watered-down Coke and I thought about kissing the boy again. As I did, I felt the back of my neck and ridges of my ears start to burn. I had that uncomfortable pressing sensation like unseen eyes were fixed on me and I quickly tried to think of something else.

For that whole year of playing together I never once talked to the boy on the wing. The most interaction we had was when I called his name out from fullback to come back for a kick return. When I turned up to training the following year and he wasn't there I felt relieved. Relieved because there was a question I had started to ask myself because of the boy. I now know that the answer to this question does not matter, but in my eleven-year-old mind it seemed to place my existence on a knife's edge between who I thought I had to be, and how I felt inside.

I think that maybe I lost a part of myself in trying to form an answer to that question because of how I felt when I looked at the boy on the wing. A softness. A tenderness. A care. Cut off and thrown away.

THE TASTE OF METAL

My forehead was pressed against the table and I held a densely clumped wad of damp tissues in my hand. I squeezed my eyes tight and felt more teardrops come out. I was thirteen.

I raised my head and saw the doctor searching for the sweet spot where his facial expressions could rest to tell me that yes, this was serious, but no, it was not the end of the world.

'Will I still be able to play footy?' I asked.

'Yes . . .' he said, 'but you, um, you can't be a pilot or a fireman.'

Mum was sitting next to me. She had one hand on my back and more tissues in the other, which she dabbed under her eyes and nose.

When Mum cried the skin beneath her eyes would swell and you could trace the line of water down the side of her face. I hold an image of her in my head—not from that day, but from years before—wearing a black hat and a red shirt, crying because she had lost her hair again. I don't know if that

37

memory is true. I feel I have constructed it. Mum would cry, though.

It was Kieren's birthday in 2007. My face was gaunt, my eyes stung like scorched desert earth under the soles of naked feet, and everything tasted like metal.

I'd lost seven kilograms and looked ill. Not sick. Ill. Sucked-in cheekbones, black under my eyes standing out against a colourless face.

I hadn't got more than a few hours' sleep in the previous two weeks. I'd been running to the bathroom eight or nine times a night. When the toilet flushed I'd crouch beside the basin, tilt my head to the side, wrap my lips around the steel tap and let the water run into my mouth.

Mum took me to the GP. He pricked my finger and pushed blood into a machine and when it beeped he said I should go straight to the hospital. I called Dad in the car. He said the same thing had happened to him when he was thirteen. I think he was lying to comfort me.

Overnight I was put on a drip. The liquid felt cold going into my arm. Every hour or so a nurse would come in and prick the tip of my finger and push blood out into a little machine. Then there would be silence until the machine would beep. When it did, I would ask: 'Does that mean I don't have it?' She wouldn't respond.

The next day we sat in a faintly lit room at Westmead Children's Hospital: Mum, Rick—the educator—and me. Rick was demonstrating.

'You put the needle on the pen, like this. Twist it, like so, dial up two units, push it out, then give the amount of insulin you need.'

I was watching, but not really.

'NovoRapid acts fast,' Rick said. 'Lantus stays in your system for twenty-four hours, so take it at night before you go to bed.'

Insulin dripped out the end of the thin metal needle. It smelt like cat piss and bleach.

Rick said I'd have to inject myself five times a day for the rest of my life with a clear liquid that everyone else's body just produced, and that I'd have to prick my finger before every meal, push blood out, and wait for a number like the nurse had done for me the night before. From then on I was to live between two numbers: four and eight. The *normal* range for everyone else, and I now had to put a needle on the end of a pen and stick it in my stomach to be *normal*.

Dad wasn't there. He was in Queensland getting his head punched in by 'The Axe', Trevor Gillmeister, in an old boys' State of Origin fight night. They called themselves the FOGS, which stood for Former Origin Greats. I jokingly called them a group of 'has-beens' and told Dad to let go of the past. He'd respond by saying, 'better than a never-was' or 'better than a never-gonna-be'.

I had asked him not to go to Queensland on the drive to school a few days earlier. We were in his green Commodore, a car that I hated because of how much it stood out. If its colour wasn't bad enough, the licence plate read 'ETHICS'. Whenever Dad drove me to school I'd duck my head when we drove past a group of girls at a bus stop on David Road. One year I asked Dad to sell the licence plate as my birthday present.

'You shouldn't go,' I said on the way to school. 'What if something bad happens to me?'

I'd always had this terrible feeling that something would happen to me after I turned thirteen. I convinced myself I had triskaidekaphobia, like a casino hotel elevator. I wished the number didn't exist; there's no logical reason for it. I just wanted to skip right over thirteen, and hoped Dad would see my dread and stay home. So I asked him not to go. He gripped the wheel between the middle and ring fingers of his right hand, his index finger running along the side of the wheel.

'We need the money,' he said.

———

After my diagnosis I was released from hospital and a few days later I was back at training with the Bulls. I was the first one there and my coach told me how his best mate had diabetes and would flick his needles up in the air and land them in his leg.

'That's cool,' I said, not really wanting to turn this new thing of mine into a game.

I don't remember anyone asking why I'd missed our last game. Maybe they were just trying to make me feel normal. Maybe it wasn't a big deal to them. Maybe it wasn't a big deal. Or maybe they didn't know, or didn't care. I thought that was fine because I didn't really want them to know.

When training started, we ran our plays on six cones enclosing the dry grass between the try line and the in-goal. Red was an inside ball. Blue was a double red. White was a cut-out pass.

Dad would always tell me how important playing 'natural' was. He said too many halfbacks were robots who didn't read the line. He hated left- and right-side playmaking, and how halfback and five-eighth had become the same position. They called the plays before looking at the numbers, and stuck to their side of the field, and threw long spiral passes as soon as they had the ball in their hands. 'Take the ball to the line,' Dad would tell me. 'No one takes it to the line any more.'

I stood on the cone at the front of the line and called red but threw to the outside player. When we ran through, Leroy, the player I'd dummied to, asked what the hell I was doing. Leroy had an earring in his earlobe and his sister was on that beer ad where the guy at the bar says, 'Four Cougars, thanks' when she turns around.

'Improvising,' I said. 'Sometimes we won't run the play we call. Don't be a fucking robot.'

The following weekend we played out at Seven Hills, and on the way to the game I started crying.

'You don't have to play, darling,' said Mum. 'We can turn around and go home, it's okay.'

The lights on the side of the road were beaming into the car; cold mist touched the windows.

'No,' I said. 'I'm playing.'

And we kept on driving down the road until we reached the ground.

In the sheds before the game I sat in the corner and checked my blood. The numbers in the middle of the machine started counting down and I shielded the monitor with my legs so no one else could see.

TRESPASSERS WILL BE PROSECUTED

I played my last game of rugby league on Leichhardt Oval in 2008. We won by fifty-something points. I'd once again followed Rhys into a different league competition. He hadn't made the Parramatta rep sides, so he moved to the Balmain competition, which he then represented in Harold Matthews Cup and SG Ball squads. Our new footballing home became the North Ryde Hawks.

I can't remember touching the ball during this final game, or even wanting to. I can't even remember who our opponent was. I just remember that it was a bright day and that I felt tired. The kind of tiredness that makes it hard to smile, or laugh, or care. The kind of tiredness where you just want to go and lie in bed. A heavy kind of tiredness. I didn't even have butterflies before the game—I felt numb, which, in hindsight, was not a numbness, but a feeling of freedom, as I was no longer feeling constantly weighed down by the future because I knew this was going to be my last game of rugby league. I didn't know how, or when, I was going to tell my parents, but I knew I was going to say: no more.

It feels fitting—deeply poetic, almost—that I ended my relationship with rugby league on the same ground where Dad would bring people to their feet when the ball was in his hands. Whenever our family went to games there, the women at the gate would usher us inside even if we didn't have tickets. Then we'd walk around and have people recognise Dad and ask for a photo or an autograph. When the siren sounded, Dad would find a way to walk into the changerooms, as though he himself still had a locker.

Leichhardt Oval is one of the remaining true suburban football grounds. The hillside beneath the man-operated scoreboard provides a nice repudiation of the ever-increasing size of electronics and nosebleed-causing grandstands that football stadiums have become. There is an excess at the top level, a constant reminder that the game is a business, with advertisements staring you in the face and lights flashing while the voiceover announces the teams. It all detracts from the game on the field. Leichhardt Oval still has an innocence to it, one that fights against the commercialisation of sport.

My final year of rugby league was for a team that was not really a team. We were a mix of kids still under the thumb of our parents, rugby union players who were looking for something to do on Sundays, and a couple of boys who were playing because it gave them the chance to hit someone.

At my first session, Evan Tuckwell, one of the boys I went to school with, asked what position I was going to try out for.

'Five-eighth,' I said.

He raised his eyebrows while jumping over the fence. 'Hmmm, wow, that's Ryan's spot. Good luck.'

There was no cohesiveness to the team—we didn't know each other, we didn't hang out after games, we didn't go on camps. Sometimes there would only be three of us at training, so we'd stand in a triangle twenty metres apart and kick a ball to one another. I'm sure our coach Jehad felt like he was just heading up an after-school day-care centre. After a game at TG Millner Field, our lock forward, Joey, who had a moustache above his upper lip and a mullet that went midway down his back, tried to fight one of our opponents. A few of us held him back while he screamed, 'YOU FUCK YOUR OWN MUM, YOU FUCK YOUR OWN MUM, CUNT!' The other kid was laughing. There was a genuine anger to Joey's screams, a frightening timbre and intensity that I can still hear.

I remember one game I was named at lock, and my mum went to find Jehad and had an exchange with him. I could hear it all from the sheds.

'That's not where he plays! He's not putting his head in the back of a scrum!'

'He's not playing the traditional lock role,' Jehad tried to explain. 'He's going to play more of a Greg Bird playmaking role—it'll suit him.'

'No. He's not playing lock. You have a duty of care!'

I played lock that day. I scored a try and set one up and was our best player.

That was the year I knew I didn't want to play rugby league any more. It started, like most, around March, with the question: 'Who are you going to play for this year?' followed by a trip to the shops to try on a new pair of footy boots. In 2008 it was white leather XBlades with red accents.

I spent Tuesdays and Thursdays convincing myself that the grey clouds overhead were heavy with rain. 'The council will close the grounds,' I'd say to anyone who would listen, and one morning I woke up pretending that I couldn't move my neck so that I wouldn't have to play. Mum could tell I was acting, and I ended up taking the field later that day.

I never questioned if footy itself was the issue, because footy was as inseparable from everyday life as blinking my eyes or taking a breath. I just thought it was the type of footy I was playing that was getting me so down, and so I began experimenting with Aussie rules, mainly because Kieren was becoming a household name with his early success at the Sydney Swans.

Kieren had become the poster boy for rugby league converts in the ongoing code war that dominated the eastern states of Australia. So after school, I started taking an old beaten-down Sherrin that Kieren had left behind over summer, plus a rugby league ball, out the front where I would kick them at the 'Trespassers will be prosecuted' sign fixed to the crosshatched wooden fence across the road. The rugby league ball was a cloaking device—a veil which could conceal my true intentions. If someone saw me kicking a Sherrin, my plan was to say that I was comparing how far each ball flew for a school science experiment. I spent most afternoons running barefoot between our front yard and this fence to collect the footies as they rolled away. Every now and then the sign would fall off and I would use the underside of my fist to punch its nails back into the slat.

At the start of the following year I left a pink post-it note stuck to the desk in my room with 'AFL Rego' written on it and the closing date below. I knew my mum would see it and bring it up. In the car home from school one day she asked me what I wanted to do about football that year and I pushed the conversation aside because I still wasn't ready.

That evening we sat at the dinner table. Dad looked at me and said, 'So, is there something you want to tell me?'

Mum was sitting in her spot to the right of me. I wanted to look at her as if to say, 'Why the fuck did you tell Dad?', but instead I looked down at my meal. Two sausages, mashed potatoes and little circles of steamed carrots.

After dinner we went out the front and Dad said I could play Aussie rules if I beat him in a golf chipping contest. Dad spent hours out the front each night, chipping golf balls at the letterbox across the road. He had a white leather bag filled with an assortment of old golf balls—Srixons, Callaways and cracked yellow Dunlops from the driving range—which he would unzip and tip on its side. He would reach in with his sand wedge, rake out a ball, have a few practice swings at three-quarter pace and then hit it at the letterbox.

Dad could drive a ball 250 metres. He had big meaty fore-arms and his torso uncoiled with ferocious torque, sending the ball off the tee on an upwards trajectory towards the sky. But he lacked the softness that a short game required. He tried different clubs, focused on holding his head down in his follow-through, gripped the club differently, but nothing worked. He'd choke down on the club and skim it. As a golfer, I was the opposite of my father. I can rarely hit a long ball, but have always had a good short game. As a fourteen-year-old I won a year's supply of Red Bull at the Jack Newton Classic against a mishmash of celebrities and Pro-Am golfers. When I walked up the front to collect my prize there were laughs in the crowd, and someone yelled out, 'Are kids even allowed to drink Red Bull?!'

Golf was something that divided Dad and me. Whenever we played golf together, usually at 5.30 in the morning on Sundays in summer out at North Ryde, it would quickly descend into a fight, then I'd drag my heels and he'd tell me to get over it. I'd be crying by the third tee and swear at him and say how much I hated golf, but that night I'd be cleaning my club heads with a toothbrush thinking that maybe next week I'd be better. Dad always said I had the golfer's build, but I just don't have the mind for golf. Before I even hit the ball I'm thinking about how bad the shot will be.

That night out the front of our house I won the chipping contest against Dad.

If he'd won I know he wouldn't have stopped me playing Aussie rules. I don't know how me saying I wanted to play no football at all would've gone down. The thought didn't even cross my mind then.

Australian rules football reinvigorated me that first year because it was something new, something in which I had *potential*. The game naturally suited me: I was quick, and with the big oval field there was space to run. My kick was a work in progress, but I spent hours upon hours each day kicking at the sign across the road.

I constantly tinkered with my kicking technique. One day I'd be holding the ball like Gary Ablett Jnr (middle fingers perfectly down the side seams, the points always towards the sky and the ground, ball dropped with a bent arm, and a focus on being compact when kicking), the next I'd mimic Ben Cousins (hands lower down the ball, and more towards the front as well, the ball parallel to ground when raised but then spinning into place when dropped). I also copied Lance Franklin's arc in my goalkicking routine, which as a rugby player who was used to kicking round the corner felt natural, and I had printed out a frame-by-frame dissection of Brendan Fevola's set shot routine, which I practised in front of the mirror in my parents' bedroom. Every time I tried a new technique I'd convince myself that it was the one. And it'd work for a while, then I'd have a few bad kicks and would start tinkering again.

For the first time in many years I found joy in sport. I enjoyed going to training and playing games, not least because I was better at Aussie rules than rugby league. By age sixteen I was playing against grown men every week in prems and leading my seniors side in goalkicking; I was up there in the league's Best and Fairest, and was also playing games for the Swans reserves.

But there were still parts I didn't like. Mainly rep teams and state camps; playing with teammates I didn't know and the general selfishness of talent identification trial games. As the prospect of getting drafted loomed, and the stages towards professionalism dominated conversations, I could feel something inside me calling out to stop again.

I had received letters of interest from Port Adelaide and Geelong. They asked me to fill out questionnaires online, and I deliberately sabotaged myself in a discreet way by making it clear I wasn't going to be a good fit at a football club. One of the recurring questions in these questionnaires was where did I see myself in five and ten years, and I answered that in five years I wanted to be studying law full-time, and in ten years hoped to have opened a law firm. If you're in recruiting, and wanting a football player, that's not something I imagine you want to hear. A player being too ambitious off the field means they won't be able to commit on it.

I had thought about telling my parents multiple times that I didn't want to play any kind of footy anymore. The closest I ever came to doing so was during a game for the Swans reserves up in Brisbane. Without a touch to half-time, I stood in a bathroom cubicle with my phone and typed the message, 'I'm done.' I had tears in my eyes. My thumb hovered above the keyboard, knowing that sending it would bring about a conversation that would give me an out. But then I stopped, walked out of the cubicle, quietly put my phone back in the side of my football bag and joined the rest of my teammates in the huddle. I could never bring myself to say those words out loud, or even send them via text. I always felt as if I were standing on top of a building looking down, but too scared to jump.

L'APPEL DU VIDE

Two weeks before the AFL State Draft Combine, I ran a practice three-kilometre time trial on the footpaths near my home. I'd measured the track out on Google Maps, meticulously, down to the metre, and decided that an out-and-back method would be the fairest, so that every hill I ran up I would eventually run back down. I started on the front lawn where the ball of Kieren's that Dad had booted came to rest years earlier. Standing at the start of the path, I shook my legs out and made sure I was as ready as possible by taking deep breaths to fill my lungs. Then I looked down, held my starting position and clicked my watch.

The sound of my shoes hitting the pavement was like a deadened metronome. Thud, two, three, four. Thud, two, three, four. Thud, two, three, four. Thud . . .

I was approaching the point where I was settling into my pace when a voice started talking. At first it was quiet. *Why are you doing this? Just stop. This is a waste of time.*

Then the voice started screaming. *JUST FUCKING STOP, THIS IS A WASTE OF FUCKING TIME. FUCKING STOP. FUCK-ING. STOP.*

My legs stopped and I put my hands on my knees and started dry-heaving. The watch read forty-six seconds. I turned around and walked back home.

———

We sat at home watching the AFL Draft on the TV. It was just background noise for me, and when the broadcast finished and my name hadn't been called out I wasn't upset. Instead there was this quiet sense of respite, a feeling that I was free. I woke up the next day and didn't even think about football. There was no heartbreak, no sobbing, no desperate longing to have it back.

I spent that next morning applying for retail jobs at Castle Towers Shopping Centre. I was excited by the proposition of working in a Target, or Kmart, or Myer. I could work out the back and stack shelves, and come home each night knowing I had a bit more money to my name than the day before. That afternoon, after seeing a physio for a general check-up, I started thinking about which university I would go to and where I might like to travel: Europe, America, one of those places where people go when they decide to self-discover. Then, as I drove along Pennant Hills Road, passing by the M2 turn off, my phone started vibrating in the cup holder beside me. I answered and put it on speaker. 'Hello . . .'

'BJ, it's Peter Berbakov from the Sydney Swans. How are you going?'

'I'm fine thanks, how are you?' The words stirred from the butterflies in my stomach and worked their way around the fingers that were in my mouth.

'That's good. Hey, has Smithy told you you're coming in to train with us on Monday, mate?'

I can't remember the rest of the conversation. But when I got out of the car I walked through the front door of our house, past the jerseys in the entranceway and the photos in the stairwell to the left, and I went into the backyard. I picked up a Sherrin and threw it against the brick wall in the backyard, which made the kitchen window rattle. The ball bounced unpredictably back to me and I scooped it up. I set out to do this a hundred more times without fumbling; each time I lost control I would start again from zero. The ball made a dull thud every time it hit the wall.

PART II

FINGERS IN THE DIRT

I drove to the Sydney Cricket Ground, the home of the Sydney Swans Football Club, the night before my first day training with them. It took eight minutes from where Kieren—and now I—lived in Randwick. At twenty-six, Kieren had just bought his second property—a three-bedroom house near the Army Barracks, next door to a family with two young girls, the elder of whom would run up and down the hallway and sometimes peer over the wooden fence into our backyard.

This is the AFL player model. Make enough money while playing to buy a property or two, so that after footy you don't have to stress about security. While people in the Real World were studying, or clawing to get internships and starting from the bottom rung of their workspaces, we were in an industry where big money was available early.

Rhys—who had lived with Kieren the year before in his apartment between Randwick Racecourse and the bus depot—was also living with us. He had a desk pressed against the wall of his bedroom, facing away from the window which looked out at our neighbour's fence less than a metre away.

Before I got into the car that night I looked up the directions and said them out loud to myself. There were six turns in total between our house and the SCG. After the fourth you were on Anzac Parade and could see the light towers that looked down upon the footy ground.

Sydney can be notoriously difficult to navigate, but it was a pretty easy route to remember. Still, I had Google Maps on beside me as a safety net. I've never been a confident driver. It took me six months to get behind the wheel after I got my Ls.

When I arrived, I sat with the engine running, looking at the bronze statue of Paul Kelly out the front of the footy club. The clock on the dash of my car was running five minutes fast, as usual. Football time is five minutes ahead, so you're never late.

I sat for a while, then drove back home, assisted by Maps once more. Before going to bed I set two alarms for the morning five minutes apart, made sure the volume of my phone was high, and repeated the route to myself once again. Canberra Street . . . straight . . . Perouse Road . . . left . . . follow Barker . . . two sets of lights . . . right . . . Botany . . . straight . . . straight . . . Alison . . . left into the right lane . . . follow past the racecourse . . . get to Anzac Parade . . . turn right . . . stay far right . . . right at Lang Road . . . left lane . . . left . . . Driver Avenue.

———

I was the first to turn up at the club, and had to wait out the front. I'd arrived at 6.30am; training started at 8.30. I have a form of time anxiety—I've always struggled to see the minutes between 6.30 and 7.30. To me they could disappear in an instant, so preparing for the worst-case scenario is my default. I was always the first to training. First to school. First to sleepovers. First to cafés. First to everything, and I'm always waiting around.

I stood on my own out the front for fifteen minutes before the next person arrived. I was checking my phone every minute to make sure I hadn't missed a message or call.

Gary Rohan walked down the footpath wearing denim shorts frayed with precision to look imprecise and tattered. The hanging threads led my eyes down to the scar on his leg. I'd been a spectator at the game where he broke it against North Melbourne, and they showed the replay on TV that night. I turn my head away when I see injuries like that, but I always have one eye fixed to the screen. I'm both disgusted and intrigued to see how much damage the game can do. I think we like seeing destruction in some sadistic way. To play football, you need to have that somewhere inside you, that thirst for pain and torment, and you have to accept the chance that it could happen to you every time you take to the field. I don't wish injury on anyone, but deep down inside myself I feel the slow churning death drive at play.

Gary rounded the corner past the ticketing box. 'Hey-o, 'ere he is,' he said.

I was too scared to talk, so I exhaled through my nose loudly and smiled. I had met Gary a few times before, but now we were training together and I felt like I was being sized up by him and that I had something to prove.

'How long ya been standing here for, huh? Come on, I got ya,' he said, raising his ring of keys up to a small grey box next to the glass sliding doors. The doors slid open and we walked into the reception of the club. There was a red leather lounge next to a desk which housed a computer framed by sticky notes. Light from the outside world seeped in, dulled by the frosting of the glass wall opposite where we entered.

'So you training with us, are ya?' Gary said.

I had to talk. 'Yeah, yeah, I am . . . Hopefully no time trial today. Haha.'

That's footy talk. We all do it. If you join a team, your best bet is to litter your words with self-deprecation and down-talk. 'Hopefully no time trial' was my way of acknowledging the unspoken agreement between players that filters its way down through the talent pathways and local footy: that we should be cautious about showing how much we care, or at the very least, balance it with fear, because confronting fear is admirable and worthy of respect, whereas caring is a form of softness, and we are not *soft*.

Gary laughed, a sign that I had spoken his language, before pressing his keys against another grey box on the frame of another door. This one was wooden, painted red, with a steel handle on top of a steel plate. 'You'll get one of these today I reckon, talk to Berba about it,' he said, pointing to the buzzer on his key ring.

A second beep, and the door opened. On the other side was white light, the kind of white light you see in hospital corridors. It lead to a decline of red-carpeted stairs. The edge of each step was lined with grooved rubber held in place by an angled slat of thin metal which collected grass off the bottom of footy boots. The brick walls either side were a clean white except for the red imprints Sherrin leather had left on them, and the bottom of the stairwell was pitch black.

We walked down, Gary a step ahead, our footsteps echoing around us.

On our descent we triggered a sensor. A light flickered on. The Sydney Swans logo appeared on the wall.

———

Less than two months earlier I'd been in the crowd watching the Swans win the Grand Final at the MCG. Late in the game Kieren beat two Hawthorn defenders to kick a crucial goal. Then Adam Goodes kicked one from the boundary. And in the dying seconds an off-balance Nick Malceski kicked a high-flying snap to seal the game. The roar of the crowd was unlike anything I'd ever heard before. It was my first taste of a packed MCG crowd. The difference between Melbourne footy crowds and Sydney footy crowds is obscene. There's a deep-seated tribalism in Victoria that has been preserved and passed down for generations. I think at any game everyone in the crowd wants to be on the other side of the fence, if only for just a moment. I've met CEOs who earn far more than any football player could ever hope, and they say they'd trade it all for a career on the field, some even for a single game.

I went out that Grand Final evening with the Swans team after the game. I'd turned eighteen only a few months before, and it was my first night out drinking. There was a line at the door of an underground nightclub that we walked straight into. People pointed at the players as we walked past. The bouncer gave me a wristband, and I got vodka sodas from the bar for free.

Kieren dragged me through the crowd and started introducing me to people. 'Gary, Gary!' he said.

Gary Ablett Jnr turned around and he and Kieren had a quick chat. His father, Gary Ablett Snr, was so good at footy that he was known in football parlance simply as 'God'. Kieren had tagged Gary Jnr a few times. I always felt nervous before those games. I'd be on the way to a game, and we'd be listening to the commentary on the radio, and I'd pray not to hear the name 'Ablett' called out. That's the other time I'd get butterflies: before watching Kieren play. I've never asked if he got nervous before games.

The lights were dim, the music was loud—The Temper Trap was playing over the speakers—and it was a hot mess of people. The senior team was scattered around the room with medals around their necks and their dirt-ridden jerseys from the game still on over the top of white button-up shirts. While I scouted the room I remember seeing Bulldog Moore, Nipper Gordon and Dylan McNeil—the reserves players—bouncing around and jumping on lounges while sculling their drinks. They didn't have medals around their necks but looked just as happy as everyone who did.

———

It was only the one-year to four-year players at training that first day. The bulk of the reserves players I had seen with their eyes rolling back into their heads after the Grand Final had been delisted or traded to make room for new players.

When Gary Rohan and I walked into the locker room another sensor was triggered and the lights turned on. Gary opened a red locker with number 16 on it, threw his backpack inside and then went to the bathroom. I sat on one of the wooden benches in the middle of the room and started reading a large plaque on the wall near the showers with the words *Hard, Disciplined, United* on it.

The locker room had fifty red steel school lockers arranged in a rectangle. On each locker were names with credentials beneath them. Tony Lockett. Paul Kelly. Bob Skilton. Barry Round. A premiership, a hundred games, a Best and Fairest, an All-Australian. If you had one of those you'd have your name preserved in white lettering on your playing locker forever.

While I was taking it all in a man appeared in front of me, wearing shorts and a visor.

I heard Gary say, 'Woah, ho, Nick-oh' as he walked back into the room.

The man replied with 'G'day Gazza,' before he extended his hand to me. 'Hey mate, I'm Nicko, how's it going?'

'BJ,' I said. 'I'm good. Excited to train.' I forced a smile again, trying to match my facial expression to the words I was saying.

Gary called out, 'That's Kizza's little brother.'

Nicko looked at me and smiled. 'Ah, right, awesome to have you in here. I'll get you some training gear. What size shorts and singlet do you reckon you'd be?'

'Probably a small,' I said.

I weighed 72 kilograms at the time. I'd never touched weights. Large clothes made me look smaller and I didn't want them to think I was a kid.

'Gotcha,' he said. Nicko clicked his fingers and walked off with enthusiasm. When he returned he handed me a pile of gear folded in clear plastic packages. Two training singlets, two pairs of shorts and a few pairs of white ISC ankle socks.

'There you go, mate. And I'll grab you a towel too,' he said.

Towels were a valuable commodity in that locker room. They were always striped white and blue, and I came to learn that it wasn't unusual for blokes to steal yours and use it for themselves or store spares in the tops of their lockers where no one could find them.

The locker room gradually filled with more players. They greeted each other with nicknames and back slaps, then threw their bags into their lockers, where their new gear was waiting for them. They'd rip open a pair of shorts, a singlet and a shirt and inspect them with a keen eye, comparing it to what they had previously worn. When they put it on they'd stretch it down and move their shoulders to get it sitting right.

I sat quietly in the middle of the room. I'm not good at introductions. I knew the names of most the guys in the room. I saw Luke Parker and Alex Johnson, who were premiership players only a couple of years older than me. As was Lewis Jetta, who pulled a small can of Red Bull from his bag which he placed on the top shelf of his locker. Ruckman Sam Naismith from the Swans Academy and North Shore Bombers sat near me, and Dan Robinson—whom I'd played juniors against and state footy with—was on the other side of him. Dane Rampe walked in with more confidence than any of the other new players. I had played him in the semifinal of the Sydney AFL Premier Division comp a few months earlier. He had gone on to win the Phelan Medal in that comp. Ramps, at twenty-two, was far more mature in his body and demeanour than me.

As I watched players come in I saw them stop at the white-board at the entrance of the changeroom to look at a piece of paper held there by two button magnets. With their finger they'd trace down to their name, then follow the line across. When no one else was standing near it I went up and looked for my name.

'Jack, Brandon: 40-minute skills, 2 × 10-minute fartleks.'

At the top of the sheet were the drills we were doing: Off the fence. Kick lanes. Tram-line kick. They were all skills drills. Nothing competitive. I looked at what the rest of the team was doing. Next to new draftees' names it said '10-minute jog'.

The draftees were Dean Towers, Harry Marsh, Matt Dick and Tim Membrey, and without even knowing them I convinced myself that I didn't like them. In my head these guys had it easy by virtue of being drafted. I was obsessed with the story of Tom Brady who went pick 199 in the NFL draft and is now considered the greatest NFL quarterback of all time, and I told myself that this could be me. There are only a few sporting archetypes that we strive to become, and I saw being written-off as integral to becoming the underdog who wins it all.

There was another sheet of paper on the board with all our names. At the top were blocks of yellow, orange and red. I looked down at a tray full of empty plastic specimen cups with yellow lids. Next to them were some already filled with urine and numbers written on the top in black texta.

'You gotta piss in the cup so we can see how hydrated you are,' said a Scottish voice coming from a blonde-haired woman with big bright teeth and red cheeks. Her name was Lorraine and she wore gloves as she dipped a thermometer-looking device into the cups of piss that were already filled.

I went to my bag and got my water bottle and started sculling water. Then I took my specimen cup and filled it to the brim with urine. I wrote 'BJ' on top with one of the textas and placed it next to the rest of the samples, all differing shades of yellow.

At 8.00am a whistle blew from down the hall. I heard someone yell out, 'Let's go boys!' Heads turned, and bodies started funnelling through the corridor, shoulder to shoulder, down towards the coaches' room. I followed and found a seat at the back. The room was filled with leg-shaking nervousness.

———

The grass on Lakeside was freshly cut. It flipped up and rested on my ankles as I ran a warm-up lap. I was wary not to run too fast because I knew long-distance running wasn't my strength and I didn't want to fall behind in the back half of the session.

When I made it back past the goal posts I saw Kenny—the white-haired old man who punched his fists in the air in the middle of the team song—standing underneath a tarpaulin.

'Young Braaannnndon Jack, look at him! How's your old man going?'

I smirked and said, 'Good.'

Next to him was a table with two large esky coolers on top, one filled with water, one with Powerade or

Gatorade—whichever brand the Swans were with at the time—and a bottle of sunscreen that the boys had started to lather onto their arms and under their eyes—never on your forehead because it'll run down into your eyes and you won't be able to see while on the field—and on the ground were orange-and-black sports bras with velcro pockets for GPS units in the back which we all had to wear.

Inside the coaches' room they had welcomed us to the club, made us stand up and introduce ourselves, and then outlined what the rest of the day would look like.

'It's all about getting as many touches as we can this time of year, because there will be sessions in-season where you might get one or two kicks, so this is the time where you get the touch work in.'

After a warm-up, we started with off the fence lanes.

'Six lanes, let's go!'

We ran out and made six even groups on the white line of the centre square. The coaches started rolling ground balls towards us.

'Get down low, get your body behind it!'

'Fingers in the dirt!'

As each player ran through, the players behind them yelled out encouragement. There was constant chatter.

'Yeah, Robbo!'

'Good work, Jetts.'

'Ahhh fucking clean, yeah boy!'

I was tentative about joining in, but used the familiar 'Got your back' call whenever I had the chance.

We shifted to away ground balls. The player in front of me missed their handball so I ran and got the ball and passed it like a rugby player back to Craig Holden—Crackers—and he just watched it sail by. He had black sunnies on and tilted his head at me. 'You going to go get it?' he said.

I ran to get the ball then handpassed it to him from about a metre away.

'We don't throw in games,' he said, 'so we don't do it here.'

Crackers was a quiet figure; so quiet that I didn't know he had played football till midway through my first year at the club. And not only had he played; he had been an All Australian in 1987. When I see him now, we talk about writing and music and socio-political issues, but back then, in those early days, I was quite intimidated by him. To this day, he's got the most consistent kick of a thirty-metre torpedo I've ever seen.

After five minutes we extended out into a kicking drill. I took extra care dropping the ball onto my foot and was only swinging my leg through at about seventy-five per cent so that my kicks popped up and gave the receiver the chance to hold where they were or run and fetch it if off-target. Nervous about my ability, I would always rather just hit the target and play it safe than start a game of roulette where a dart made the coaches say 'kiiiiick' and a miss caused eyes to search for who the guilty party was. Another unspoken agreement of football training is to know your limits and play to them so that the drills continue to flow.

I was also making an extra effort to keep my arms straight and kick like an AFL player. My kick was not a natural Aussie rules kick. Years of tinkering on the front lawn have left me with a round-the-corner style rugby kick that has been beaten down, broken up and re-assembled in the likeness of who I aimed to be. At best, it's an ugly imitation.

My fingers don't feel comfortable along the seams of the ball, so instead I smother the front with my palms. I spin sideways when I kick, so that my left hip ends up facing the target on my follow-through. My support leg bends before impact. And my left arm is cocked at a right angle.

Paul Roos was always on me about the bent left arm. I never sorted it out. It might have something to do with the fact that I'm right-handed but left-footed. When I was young Kieren said to Mum and Dad that I should either become right-footed or left-handed, because my ball drop was terribly inconsistent coming from my left hand down to my left foot.

After a few drills a whistle blew for longer than any of the ones before, and Rob Spurrs yelled out, 'Righto boys, runners on!'

The mood shifted. Murmurs of 'Ahh, fucking hell, who's ready?' were met by silently raised eyebrows. Shirts came off and GPS bras were adjusted, and a few boys ran off to the bathroom.

Spurrsy—the fitness and conditioning coach—held a clipboard in his hand and explained the session to us again. 'Righto boys, we're doing two sets of fartleks,' he said. Fartlek, Swedish for 'speed play', is a form of interval running where you change your intensity after specified times or distances. It was the closest form of running training we did to actual game running. It's brutal, and yet there is still no type of running that prepares you for match fitness.

'First up, we got a Braddy,' said Spurrsy. Braddys, or Bradshaws, were a pattern of fartlek interval running made specifically for big forward Daniel Bradshaw during his tenure at the Swans because apparently that was all his body could do.

You walk from point post to point post, then jog to the junction of the 50-metre line, then stride along the boundary line till you get to the other junction. The second fartlek was a 10–20–30. 10 seconds hard. 20 seconds stride. 30 second walk.

I made an effort to run alongside Lewis Jetta for the session. There'd been a story about Kieren running with Jetts the previous off-season and they made a point of saying that it had helped make Jetts the player he was as Kieren was billed as the toughest trainer at the club.

At the end of the session, Leon, the midfield coach, walked past and said that he'd noticed what I was doing. 'It's good,' he said. 'Keep doing it.'

After the session, some coaches asked me to come over and do some one-on-ones against Dane Rampe. On the sixth or seventh lead, Ramps put his knee into my back while spoiling and I went down and started cramping. If you're a cramper, then you know as you are going down that you won't be able to stand back up.

Stuey Dew ran over and put my legs in the air and pushed down against my toes with his hand. He was laughing. I hobbled into the sheds after training and sat on the ground with a bag of crushed ice under each calf, waiting for all the boys to get out of the showers before I got in.

We did yoga at Clovelly that afternoon as a group. Lying on the wooden floorboards with my eyes closed, my body was weighed down by the training I'd done that day.

FRONT LINE

The player in front of you has the ball. Can you impact? Yes. Close in on him. GO. GO. Shorten your strides. Don't get stepped. Don't over-commit. One. Two. Three. Four. Dig up the dirt. STOP. Put your hands up. Wave your arms. What foot does he kick with? Right. He doesn't have a left. He never uses his left. Don't give him the easy one down the line. Stand in front. Get big on the mark. Make them have to kick it over you. Make sure you are loud. No, louder. NO, FUCKING LOUDER. FUCKING SCREAM, CUNT. 'I'VE GOT THE MARK, I'VE GOT THE FUCKING MARK!' Now look left. Look at the short 45s. There's movement but it's not on. Who's next to you? Talk to them. Let them know where you are. It's obvious where you are. But still, say something. Say anything. I'M HERE, I'M HERE. I GOT BALL, I GOT BALL. Talk for the sake of talking. Make noise, because noise is chaos and chaos turns over the ball. Don't be silent. Silence is bad. Never be silent on the field. Where's the ball. Still there. HEY, HEY, HEY. Try to throw them off. Now listen to where the other voices are. Don't look, you should know where they are by their voices alone. GOT YOUR BACK. I'M HERE BJ, I'M HERE. Now look at the kicker's eyes, where are they looking, where do they want to go. Long 45 first. Then short 45. Move your feet where they look. Left one step. Back right. Left again. Make everything difficult for them. That's the priority. Where's the ball. Are they ready to kick or just trying to pull you off the mark. Watch their arms for the ball drop. Once they commit, we go. We hunt. We always hunt. Hunt. In packs. Hunt them down. Hunt like a wild animal in the African wilderness. Hunt like a lion with blood dripping from its maw. They look to their right and kick sideways. That's a win. Scream out. Louder now. Don't chase the ball. Let your teammate get the mark. You pull back a few metres. Sit between the player in front who just kicked and the one behind you. What do you have? Pace. What does pace mean? Longer teasing distance. You want them to kick it back to your player. Going sideways is nothing. Give them sideways. If they kick to the guy in front, close in, go quick. Anticipate. Hunt the intercept. Hunt them down. Hunt them down. We want the fucking ball back. What's going on behind you. Don't look. Stay side-on. Always side-on with your torso facing the ball and your hands at the ready. Always be in the go position, ready to move either way. One can guard two. That's the whole premise. One can guard two. The person behind you yells out. LEFT LEFT LEFT. Don't look, just trust the voice. It's directed at you, you can tell. It means someone is leading into the short 45. The kicker's eyes shift towards them. If the ball hangs in the air, make them earn it. Crash your body into theirs like a Daytona 500 car wreck. Twisted metal and flames to the cheers of the crowd.

You take two steps to your left. Crouching. Side-on. That cuts off the lead. Now reset. Move back to where you were so the guy in front can't get the ball and play on. If they play on they'll break the lines. Defence starts with you. It starts on the front line. You're a maniac. A fucking front-line maniac. The most ruthless cunt on the field. Get the ball. Get the ball. Get the fucking ball. The whistle blows. Move it on. They kick long. GET THERE GET THERE. We force the intercept. FUCKING OATH BOY. ALRIGHT, RESET. RESET. The ball comes in. It hits the ground, PLAY ON PLAY ON. You close in on the player with the ball. Watch their hips. Watch their hips. Don't worry about the ball. Watch their hips. Steady your steps again. One. Two. Three. Four. Short. Sharp. Stutter. Steps. Their teammate wraps around for a handball. The voice from the guy to your left says HAND OVER HAND OVER. Don't cross paths, remember. Never cross paths. Guard space. Wait for them to move into your space. Team defence. But if you can impact, go. Can you impact? Can you? Step off. Acknowledge the handover. GOT IT, STAY LEFT, TAKE MINE, I GOT YOURS. You now have the guy with the ball. Press him. Quick. Get in his face. But don't get stepped. They hit a target behind you. Don't turn around, don't watch the ball, keep your eye on the man in front. Check them on the way through, put your arm up, bump him off. Nothing easy. Be a cunt. Be a real cunt. Don't let them get the post-up handball. They start to jog. They're out of the play. Can you impact? Now you slide down. Defence starts with the forwards sliding. Slide down. Don't turn your back. Talk to the mids. SLIDE DOWN SLIDE DOWN. Make sure your head's on a swivel. The mids start to move, passing the message on to the defenders. We leave the spare deepest. The ball has to hang in the air longest to go to the spare. The moment they look to kick long we push back. We out-work our opponents and that way we are free in transition. The whistle blows. Talk in your teams. Have a drink. What did we do well? We're working well in our triangles. What else? What else are we doing well? Coming forward. Yeah, we came forward to press them and it put them under pressure. If in doubt, don't hesitate, just come forward. It gets the off-ball shape going. The off-ball is a whirlpool. Players come forward on the side of the ball and the guys running back on the other side fill the space behind them. It only works if we trust it. It's our inside and outside defence working together. Don't get sucked in, but if you can impact, go. We have layers. Mechanisms. Keep getting after them. Hunt them down. The whistle blows again. Okay, back out. Blue footy. Let's go. I've got the front line. The ball is kicked. Can you impact? Yes. Close in on them. Fucking close in.

HARD, FAST, CLEAN

Journal entries from 2013

January 9th

Had the AFL Player induction camp for three days. I learned some valuable lessons. Ben Graham (former Geelong captain and then NFL punter) asked two main questions: 'How professional are you?' and 'How do you want to be remembered?'

Sunday night we had to get our own dinner. I got Chinese and this completely fucked me over and I've been sick since. No appetite, no energy. I had to miss training today as well. Moral of the story—be a fucking professional. If I want to play AFL football I have to care about my own priorities. As Mum said, all those other guys would take your spot like *that*.

We did 3 × 10-minute fartleks at the Botanical Gardens. I threw up afterwards. I never throw up after running.

I will do the extras every day. Extra touch sessions. Extra ice baths + stretches. Extra tapes—watch individuals and learn how everyone around you plays and how you will get the ball. Extras on game plan. Gym extras—push-ups and biceps every day. Let everyone see you doing extras so they all will come to respect you.

February 12th

Spoke to John Longmire [seniors coach]. He says he's been very impressed—even surprised—at how well I'm doing. He's unsure if I'll play NAB Cup because of my size (bullshit, by the way). Things to work on: working around oppo body work; always step and burn opponent. Execute skills more precisely.

February 14th

Valentine's Day. Got a rose for Georgia.

PRACTICE GAME TOMORROW FOR 60 MINS. I will work my fucking arse off. Get front and squares; no fly-bys. Own the stalker role. Wait and pounce, then tackle hard. Use pace. Kick well.

Goal: 3 goals, 12 touches, 3 chase-down tackles, 3 turnovers from stalker.

Tomorrow I give them no option but to play me in NAB round one.

February 20th

Selected on bench for NAB round one against Carlton and GWS. So happy to tick off a goal already. I'll do my best to make a good impression.

Swans players induction night. Leadership group took all the first-year players to middle of SCG to watch some highlights of 2012 season. Bloods footy is relentless pressure and hardness. Then we walked around the oval imagining what it will be like to play in front of a packed crowd one day.

March 7th
Pulled from training as my markers were down. Fucking livid. That's a missed chance to make a statement. Need to do more recovery. Extra stretching, additional ice baths every day.

March 15th
Practice game vs Sydney Hills Eagles. Starting as half-forward but will rotate through midfield.

Goals: Be in and under. Be hard at the footy, make them all go, *Shit he's not just quick, he's fucking tough*. 3 tackles a quarter. Forward pressure must be high. Kick goals from forward pressure. Be loud, lead up for short 45s, remember you are a good lead-up player, don't just crumb. Feed off Mitch Morton, get front and square, and be a leader. Be a leader.

March 24th
Game last Friday vs Sydney Uni. We won by 200 points. Craig Bird, Marty Mattner, Shane Mumford, Nick Smith, Mitch Morton all played. I kicked 3 goals but need to kick inside 50 faster. Morto had a go at me about it on field, but next kick I set him up for a goal. I must improve hands in marking contests.

March 25th

Had a development group Leading Teams session today. We all sat in a circle and gave feedback to each other. What I need to improve on: building relationships with all the guys, getting around the boys.

Weekend's game: 3 goals, 13 touches, 8 tackles, 12,640m at 140m/min (highest).

March 29th

Game vs GWS tomorrow. Season officially starts.

Be the hungriest, hardest cunt on the field. There's a senior spot open and you fucking want it. Have 12 pressures and 4 goal assists. Tackle hard. At a contest, if you are inside just tackle the man with the ball. Stalk. Use your voice, demand the footy, make yourself big. Attack the footy. Forward entries: if at 50 hit the top of the square. Look inboard, pull the trigger. Push off the mark hard and fast.

March 31st

Wasn't a good game for me. I was so lost. Caught in no-man's-land. Had 4 touches, 1 goal.

What I need to do: if you can impact, have a fucking crack—you didn't get to enough contests. Push and shove in there. Be aggressive and hunt the ball. Don't get caught too far up, let someone else stalk if past halfway, make sure you work hard back inside 50. Sprint, don't stride.

April 10th

Dad sat me and Kieren down and told us that Rhys opened up to him (first time they've really spoken in 12 months). Rhys said he was sick of the pain caused by football and the resentment he had because he is no longer playing. All he wanted to do growing up was play for Australia and he feels like he's let us down. I love Rhys no matter what he does; I feel like giving up football myself so he doesn't feel alone. At least he's opened up—we can help him move forward.

April 15th

Weekend's game vs Tuggeranong. Won by 193 points. 21 disposals, 3 goals 1. Morton kicked 11, Walsh 7, Membrey 3. Positives: work rate, clean hands, leading patterns. Improvements: reaction time. Development meeting: I was the highest first-year player who shows Swans trademark. Tom Mitchell, Tim Membrey and Marshy voted for me. My trademark: disciplined, determined, trusted.

May 9th

Was Hill from Hawthorn in 18 vs 18 today. He pretty much just piss-bolts forward from stoppages. It's a good sign being a target player in 18 vs 18. Coaches noticing all the extra goalkicking I'm doing. Went in to the SCG yesterday and had 100 shots. It's all about feel. Still, I lost to Goodesy and Dicky in a goalkicking contest and had to serve them lunch.

May 15th

Did extras with development boys today. Yesterday Nick Davis went through my tape and said that I have something our first-grade forward line doesn't have: pace, and that I must use it as much as I can. Stuey Dew said that in all the meetings it's been brought up that I do my role and stick to structures and that, again, I have the speed which we lack.

Macca walked into the changeroom with Kizza and said, 'Speak of the devil, we were just talking about you.'

Kieren said my name was with Tom Mitchell and Jake Lloyd's as an almost-emergency.

Use my pace. Tomorrow, take blokes on. Chase them down.

May 17th
Tomorrow I will be loud on the field, talk to mids as stalker, direct forward line; be a leader. Use my pace, be clean (slow and steady), then burst away and have a bounce. Chase-down tackles. Chase down everything that moves, manic pressure. Kick goals. Back yourself in.

May 20th
Had an MRI on my knee today. Physios and doc think I've hurt my PCL. Was in the doc's room with Jetts when he was told he won't play this weekend. Is this my chance?

May 21st
MRI scans showed my PCL is ok. Still a lot of fluid, though. Doctors said they might have to drain it. Did a ten-minute run, felt fine. All the coaches kept asking how I was. People calling me tough for playing on a PCL. Davo hinted I should walk

down the hallway to see the senior coaches. No word as yet, but I am in the mix.

May 27th

19 Disposals. Tom Mitchell had 56. A lot of bullshit easy ones, though. Tim Schmidt once had 63 and Matty O'Dwyer had a few 60+ games. Kizza said I shouldn't play that way. But how will I distinguish myself from players like that? 1. Chase-down tackles, 2. Run and use my pace. Make my ten touches more memorable than their 40.

May 29th

Day off. Did a 30-minute bike, goalkicking, and practised running and bouncing. At training yesterday we were doing the L.O.G. (length of ground) skill drill and Nick Davis was defending. He told me to get the ball, run and kick the goal from 50 (as opposed to hitting a target). He deliberately gave me space and I slotted it. Also got a chase-down tackle (love it).

Meeting with Horse [John Longmire, seniors coach] yesterday. He said I'm doing really well and I've got something the team could really use. I just have to improve my tank. Goal is to wreck myself this off-season, come back fit as fuck.

18 vs 18 tomorrow, take them on.

May 31st

I am hard, clean, fast. Tomorrow I will have relentless pressure, and chase everything down. I'll use my pace to break the game open. Run and bounce.

June 2nd

Game vs Belconnen yesterday. 7 shots at goal (3.3 and one out on the full), and set up another 2. Named in the best. Peter said to me as I walked off: 'At this rate you'll be playing senior footy very soon.' Had a great chase-down tackle in front of all the boys—really used my pace and backed myself.

June 5th

Text today from the club saying, 'From John Longmire: you are required to attend the team meeting tomorrow morning.' Then I received a call from Horse as I was about to jump-start my car. I'm a chance to play first grade. I have to get through training okay, and then they have to promote me to the senior list by 4pm tomorrow.

June 6th

At the age of 19 and 5 days I will make my debut for the Sydney Swans. Trained the house down. Kicked a goal and had other dangerous touches in 18 vs 18. If I can do it against the Swans I can do it against anyone.

John Longmire spoke to me on the field, jokingly. Said, 'Thought you were shithouse today.'

Was eating lunch in the lounge and Kieren comes up and said, 'What did you do at training, Horse is furious.' We walked into the boardroom together and Horse was sitting in front of the whiteboard. Horse: 'You can tell him, Kizza.' Kizza: 'You're playing your first senior game this weekend. You're here because you're disciplined, and because you listen.'

Horse: 'I think you can be a really good player for this club.'
I signed paperwork straight after and was elevated to the
senior list.

Leon said, 'The best thing you did was stay strong and say you
weren't injured.'

Nothing changes—just play my normal game.

June 7th

I play my first senior game tomorrow. I'm a bit nervous, but
I feel if I just keep playing to my strengths I'll be fine. When on,
apply relentless pressure, chase them down, be a maniac with
your efforts. Hard. Fast—back yourself, take space. Clean.

I am hard.
I am fast.
I am clean.

Relentless forward pressure (10 × one-percenters). I am the
impact player.

June 8th

Went to Mark Ricciuto's nightclub after the game. I'm pretty
fucked right now. Had two jugs of vodka Red Bull.

June 20th

Playing reserves on the weekend. Reasons: need match fitness,
and if Tippo pulls up sore in his first game they think Lamby
will be able to run out the game better.

What I've learned: I can hold my own at AFL level, but I need to get fitter. Must be clean. Back my assets.

What I do next: Keep good form in reserves—you are a leader out there. Attack the reserves game—you are in good form, now take it to the next level again and prove a point. Attack all training sessions, kill 18 vs 18, do extras, be hungry. Give them no choice. Be the most electrifying player on the field.

June 23rd
Lost to NT by 50 points. We had 8 local top-ups play for us who we'd never met. Me: 18 disposals, 2 goals, 2 goal assists, 6 tackles. Peter refuses to name me in the best even though it was obvious that I was our best.

August 15th
Right now I feel depressed. I feel no one loves me. I see no point in anything. I feel lonely. I am playing reserves on the weekend. Let's prove a point.

WHEN THE LAKE FREEZES OVER

After making my debut midway through 2013, I played another eight games of seniors that year. I had unexpectedly overtaken all the boys who were drafted ahead of me, and I started to thrive in the professional environment. I felt a great degree of comfort in the repetition and structure of each day, and had by and large rote-learned the footballing life.

I played for the reserves in Canberra in the NEAFL eastern conference final, which we won. They gave out a trophy and a best-on-ground medal, but it was a meaningless victory. Especially for guys like me who had an eye on the senior team. We laughed to each other on the dais while receiving the trophy, and we sung the team song with that fake, somewhat ironic, kind-of-jovial cheer that reserves players muster about their accolades—like team-of-the-year honours—which are not really accolades, but rather reminders that they are playing in the twos.

When we sat down in the sheds Peter said that he was pleased, but that there was now a bigger job at hand. Our role was to support the senior side through the rest of their season, at training and by drawing out the length of our season. All through the year Peter would remind us that his job was to create AFL footballers, not NEAFL footballers.

I found myself constantly trying to impress Peter as a coach, a task made difficult by his restraint in giving praise. But I think he was like that with most of the young guys, especially the ones who weren't defenders, and it made us work harder. When Tommy Mitchell broke the record for the most touches ever in a game of footy with 64, Peter stood up the front and made a pointed statement about how we weren't a club that valued kick-chasing, before going on to praise Xavier Richards who had something like 6 touches from full-back. He didn't mention Tommy's name, but it was very obvious who the words were directed towards. In one of our earliest development group meetings I remember he scattered a handful of red (offensive players) and black (defensive players) magnets on the whiteboard. He then drew an X where the ball was and said, 'Okay where do the defenders go?' A few boys took turns, but no one got it right. He had to piece it together for us. Even if you were right he would roll his hands in front of him and ask you to keep searching. He'd stand at the front of meetings and take answers from the floor, and after each one he would say, 'Yeah, but what else am I talking about . . .' That was just him though, always wanting more from us. Pushing us to not be content with being a reserves footballer.

I had something like 18 disposals and a goal in the game plus a hand in a few others. I had spent the year as a crumbing forward. In our first intraclub match I lined up on Nick Malceski—who had been the hero of the Grand Final three months earlier—and I hit a perfect front-and-square less than ten seconds into the game. My team got the clearance, I ripped back into the forward 50 from the centre square, didn't put on the brakes and the ball literally fell into my lap off the hands of the pack. I had a shot at goal running at full pace, which missed, but the clip was shown a fair few times in our meetings, and from then on everyone came to view me as a crumbing forward.

In reserves, however, I tended to play a more hybrid half-forward/midfield role. I rarely kicked multiple goals— I was never a natural goalkicker; I don't have that inbuilt goal sense in me—but I would usually have six or seven inside 50s and top our score involvements. I was the facilitator who got the ball inside 50. That was my strength as a footballer.

That year we had guys like Jesse White, Mitch Morton, Tommy Walsh and Tim Membrey playing deep who were all capable of kicking ten in a game at that level. They had strong hands, and were rarely out-marked, so a crumbing forward role which relies on the ball hitting the deck didn't work as well. There would be games early in the year where I'd come off with single-digit touches and no goals, but that was just how it was. I learned to adapt my role because having a game like that in a week when a senior spot opened up meant I wouldn't be in contention. I also lacked patience on the field, and to be a small forward you need to wait and trust that the opportunity will present itself, like a sniper. I would always get scared it wouldn't, so I would move myself up the ground to try to get involved. By doing so, I'd create a self-fulfilling prophecy.

In some ways reserves football was harder for me than seniors because our midfielders had more time when breaking out of stoppages and so would be able to run and kick over the half-forwards' heads. But I learned I could easily lose my opponents in transition, and that if I kept running I would eventually get the ball. One thing you learn to think about once you're on a list is where the ball goes next. You learn that if you don't react as soon as the ball is turned over, it'll come up in a meeting and your reaction time will be criticised. Those moments just after the ball has been won by either team are the moments when you get on your bike. They're what separate AFL footy players from the rest.

After the conference final, rather than catch the bus back to Sydney from Canberra, those of us who were a chance to play seniors the following week caught a plane. I stared out the window for most of the flight. I always enjoy looking down over sparsely populated parts of land. And I liked looking down at small towns with one road coming in and out, and trying to imagine what it would be like to live there. To have gone to a small school and had different friends who lived down the road and to be someone else. I feel outside of myself after thinking these thoughts for too long. Tony Armstrong sat next to me on the flight. I liked Tony because he wore paisley button-up shirts and bucket hats and went to record stores. He was the kind of guy who stood out from the usual monotony of football changerooms.

He saw me looking out the window and tapped me on the shoulder. 'So, get this,' he said. 'As a kid I used to think that clouds were like castles in the skies where people lived. It's ridiculous I know, but I was a kid.' Then he laughed his very loud and distinct cackling laugh.

I could feel cool air on my forehead from the small circular vent above me. 'Huh, that's pretty cool,' I said, moving my eyes closer to the window.

He turned back away.

I would've been fine catching the bus. I enjoyed the drive to and from Canberra—I'd done it every second weekend with Mum and Dad when Kieren played Swans reserves during his first two years at the club.

On the bus, after the initial humdrum wears off, everyone settles and does their own thing. Usually a game of cards goes on towards the back (the game is Arsehole, started by the three of spades. If you play two fives you say *good coffee*). Laptops come out. Headphones go into ears. Jumpers are folded up and used as pillows against windows which vibrate and jump in response to the road.

On return trips we'd stop at the McDonald's midway between Sydney and Canberra and take half an hour to stretch our legs while Shinpad—the bus driver—would go inside and make small talk with the workers.

When we got back on the bus, Shinpad would put a pirated DVD on for us to watch. Something like *Safe House*, or *Argo*, and then we'd turn all the lights off. If you'd played well the trip home was filled with a sense of contentment. The following week you would ride the momentum of having done what you were supposed to do. But if you'd played poorly then that drive back was the worst thing in the world. All you'd want was another game the next day so you could go out and rectify things. A week at the footy club after a bad game dragged on, and on, and on.

From what I've heard, every club has a Shinpad. They're usually in charge of the cheer squad, or the person who cleans boots before the games—a mercurial figure who no one can really place, but they'd do anything for the people at the club.

Pad worked his way up from being bus driver of the reserves to being a player masseur before senior games. He spoke with a thick eastern European accent from a country that I couldn't quite put my finger on.

'Jacky, Jacky,' he'd say to me. 'It's fookin' bullshit they not play you, fookin' bullshit. I speak to Dewy and Horse. I ask why. They say you need to kick better. Okay?'

'Okay,' I'd say. 'Thanks Pad.'

I had a real soft spot for Pad. When I started making music he said he'd be my security guard if I ever needed one. The last time I saw him was in 2018 when he drove the bus up to Kieren's bucks party. All he wanted in return was to come and have a drink with the boys, which he did. I think he's taxiing healthcare workers around these days.

———

There was always a moment of anticipation before the far right panel of the whiteboard was pulled out to reveal who was playing that week. Horse would walk over from the lectern on the other side of the room, and say something like, 'Alright, here's the squad. We will finalise it after training.'

The section where my gaze would immediately go was off to the left-hand side of the diagram of the field, where there were usually six to eight name magnets lined up, or arranged in rows, four of which would end up becoming the final four in the side, while the rest would be emergencies.

In my first year I took being the emergency as a tick against my name. To me it was a sign that I was the future of the team because the way they arranged the magnets on the board made it look like you were next in line. Eventually I realised that's not really how it works.

A lot of it depends on who's in form in the twos, who can afford to miss a week—or who they don't mind missing a week—how likely someone is to get through training or a game, and if there are regular starters coming back after injury. Guys who would slot straight back in to seniors after getting match fitness did not fill the emergency role. We had an unspoken rule that there were no golden tickets back into the team—even Goodesy played reserves at some point—but there were guys whose path avoided the non-playing emergency role because they needed to be out on the field playing so they could 'put their hand up' for selection.

The non-playing emergency role became a dreaded part of the footballing experience for me because it meant I had to do a one-on-one skills and running session early in the morning after the game so as to have done something physical that weekend. And I had to do this session knowing that I wouldn't be in proper contention to play seniors the following week, because I needed match fitness, which the one-on-one skills didn't provide. Then on Monday I'd have no gameplay of my own to review, and would be irrelevant during lunchtime conversations where stories from the weekend's games were shared and discussed. I became a wandering soul of the in-between realm that was neither seniors nor reserves.

The week after the eastern conference final, I was taken as the emergency to Perth where we were set to play Fremantle in a preliminary final at Subiaco. Reserves were playing against Brisbane in the NEAFL grand final that same weekend. I arrived at Sydney airport in a taxi with Kieren, who had just been named in the All-Australian team for the first time.

We dropped our bags off at the Virgin check-in where John Payne attached priority tags to their handles. Then we collected our travel packs of food, vitamins and drinks, and made our way to the lounge.

When I walked in I saw the coaches off on their own, newspapers and coffees in front of them, and around the corner from them the bulk of the playing group huddled around two long tables. I put my backpack on a seat then went to get a latte. I'd only just started drinking coffee. It was more of a social thing than anything else. We always had time to kill in between meetings and massages and weights, so we'd walk to Fox Studios, or Azure café, and get coffee in groups. At this stage I think I was still having two sugars in everything because my palate had not yet become accustomed to the bitterness.

When they called us for boarding I headed to the newsagency next to the gate and bought two small Cadbury chocolates and a book called *I Hope They Serve Beer in Hell*.

On the plane, Vince asked what the book was about and I said, 'It's just a bunch of stories from a guy who drinks and parties and sleeps with girls.'

'Oh, right,' he replied.

I read twenty pages while we were still on the tarmac before growing bored. I tried to sleep for the rest of the flight, but couldn't.

We landed. I rushed to the bathroom, then re-joined my teammates at the baggage claim. There were a fair few fans waiting for us at the airport.

A man wearing an unzipped hoodie and open-toed sandals approached me with a stack of playing cards held together by rubber bands. He fished through and pulled out one with my name and face on it and asked me to sign it. After I did, one of the senior boys told me to next time ask who the card was for so I could write that name at the top, otherwise these guys would just put the stuff on eBay and make money off us. I didn't really mind if they did, but I didn't say that.

People were breathing down our necks, holding guernseys and scarves—scarves were a fucking pain to sign—in their hands that they wanted our names on, and then when we weren't looking, they'd take photos of us. We didn't really have those types of fans in Sydney. We lived in a sanctuary away from the real centre of the AFL world. There was maybe one woman I can remember who after most home games would stand out the front of the SCG with a backpack on and a flag in her hand, and ask, 'Where's Goodesy?' or 'Where's Buddy?' to everyone who came out. But there was no one with a wad of cards held together by an elastic band. We called those fans 'footy horns' and joked about anyone possibly loving football that much.

As soon as my bag came out at baggage claim I ripped it off the conveyor belt and made my way towards the team bus. Everyone had specific seats which were stringently kept if you were a regular in the team. The emergencies and guys who came in and out of the team would point at a seat and ask who sat there and be met with a reply like, 'Nah, nah, that's Bolts' seat.'

Usually the emergencies wound up next to one another, behind the coaches. On this trip I took Sam Reid's spot at the back.

———

The pool at the hotel was ice cold; the shadows of the surrounding buildings enveloped it. I stood on my tiptoes with my hands wedged between my armpits and after ten minutes I got out.

It was the day before the game, so after our morning kick and recovery we had spare time till dinner. Payney had hired out three Taragos for us to take. A group of us piled in to one and went to Timezone and saw a movie before coming back for our massages.

For me, the day before a game was usually filled with trying to avoid thinking about the game. I allowed myself a few moments of visualisation—making a tackle, kicking a goal— but once I started thinking about all the different situations that could come up I would feel helpless. There was no turning it off. My entire career I was plagued by this vision of playing in the grand final. I'd be lining up for goal at a crucial part of the game and I'd kick the ground instead of the ball. I was always worried that I'd get to the biggest moment of my career and then sabotage myself. I don't know where that thought comes from, or why, but it persisted for all the years I played.

As the emergency I was always wary of falling too deeply into the mindset of playing, because it lead to a severe feeling of disappointment when the ball was bounced and I was left standing in the race, watching. But still, I always wanted to be ready in case someone went down, so I was in a constant back-and-forth, letting my mind run free and then reining it in when it wandered too far.

I'd been messaging a woman on Instagram since we'd arrived in Perth. She said she lived ten minutes away from our hotel, so I asked her to come over that night.

I caught the elevator down to the lobby after my massage and left a key card at reception for her. I couldn't go down and bring her up because we had a team rule about having company in our hotel rooms before games.

Since I'd become a professional footballer and moved out of home, I had felt a sense of inadequacy about the number of women I had slept with. At one of my first team dinners I had to stand up the front and tell the story of the first time I had sex. I was nervous. Fumbling around for words. I didn't know how to tell it. It wasn't an interesting story. We were in the same year at school. She came over one day when my parents were out. And we had sex. That was it and that's how I told it before sitting back down and feeling like I'd exposed my sexual inexperience in front of the group.

During that first year as a footballer I'd started meeting women out at nightclubs. I had learned that alcohol alleviated my anxiety in social settings and made it easier for me to talk to people I didn't know. After a couple of drinks I wasn't the quiet boy sitting in the corner any more. I was chatty, confident, a faux version of myself veiled in confidence.

The idea of talking to a woman I had never met in my hotel room while completely sober made me nervous. There were small bottles of rum and vodka in the mini-fridge which I took out and thought about drinking, but the club would always get the receipt for these. I knew there was a BWS not far from the hotel, but I just sat in my room, playing out the upcoming scenario in my head, convincing myself I could do it. Then there was a knock at the door.

I jumped up and almost tripped over the used training gear that was spilling out of my travel bag. My heart was beating right up into my mouth and my mind was questioning why I'd invited her over.

I steadied myself before turning the handle. *Why was I doing this?*

'Hey,' she said, looking up at me from the hallway. Part of me had been hoping she wouldn't turn up.

'Hey,' I replied, still gripping the handle of the half-cracked door. 'Do you want to come in?'

She smiled wryly and walked past me with folded arms, then started to look around the room. The bathroom door was shut, the curtains were open; there wasn't much to see.

'So, um, do you want a drink or something?' I asked.

'Nah, I'm alright,' she replied.

I turned the TV on so that it wasn't just our voices in the room. She perched herself on the corner of the bed and I sat towards the pillows, the flats of my feet planted down so that my knees were between my face and the rest of the room.

'So, um, how was your day?' My throat was dry, my voice coming out trebly. Young. Scared. Unsure of itself.

'Good,' she said, pausing, then running her finger in circles on the bed next to her bent knees. 'I just spent it with my little one.'

She waited for a response. Maybe a question about the kid she had just mentioned, or a raised eyebrow or something, but I didn't offer anything.

We talked for a bit—about nothing really—then she moved across the bed and put her lips on mine. While we kissed I kept thinking that I didn't want her in the room but I didn't say anything. But I also thought about how I would have a story to tell the boys after.

The apprehension I held in my mind must've made its way down to my lips because she stopped. 'Is everything okay?' she asked.

'Yeah,' I said, 'everything's fine,' and we started kissing again. I moved my hand to her waist and she started to lift up my shirt. *I don't even know this person. I don't want this. Why am I doing this.* We stopped again. She looked at me, and I know I looked at her, but in my mind today I can't see her face.

'Are you sure everything's okay?'

I can't even remember her name.

'Yeah, I'm sure, I swear.'

Or her eye colour or her hair.

'Is there . . . another girl or something?'

How her voice sounded. I can't remember any of it.

'What?'

What was her fucking name. Why can't I remember it.

'Like a girl back in Sydney?'

'Oh . . .'

She moved away and I pulled my shirt down. We lay on top of the covers with a gap between us. I took a deep breath in and pretended that the look of anguish on my face was because I was in love with another woman.

'I understand,' she said. 'I'm kind of in the same situation with a guy at the moment.'

She propped herself up on the corner of the bed again. Her feet touched the ground. A weight lifted from the room.

'Is it your kid's dad?' I asked.

'Yeah,' she said, running her fingers through her hair.

We sat and talked for a while with the TV still on in the background. I asked about her kid, and if she'd ever travelled, and she asked if I got nervous before games. 'Yeah,' I said. 'Like you wouldn't believe.'

'It must be so exciting running out in front of crowds like that, though.'

'Yeah, I guess it is.'

Eventually she said she had to go to work. I gave her a hug and offered to pay for her taxi, but she said it was fine. When the door shut I took my clothes off and had a shower. With my head pressed against the bathroom tiles I wondered if she had come here wanting to prove something, or just to be someone else for a night. Maybe, I thought. But I'd never know.

The following night I stood in the race in my warm-up kit and looked out at the ground while the boys took to the field. The goal posts at the opposite end were barely visible. We lost, had some drinks in the hotel lobby, then caught the red-eye back to Sydney.

ICARUS

I woke one Saturday morning sprawled across three plastic chairs that were fixed to the floor of the hospital waiting room. Beside me, my teammate Liam slept.

The clock, vibrating on the wall, yet to find its resting place, read somewhere between four and five am. I stood up and walked towards the woman behind the desk. 'Is there anything you can give me for this?' I asked, pointing to my lip. It hurt to talk.

'Sorry darl,' she said. 'You'll just have to wait for the doctor.'

The thin red second hand of the clock made its way around and around and around. I had to run a three-kilometre time trial in two days' time.

I'd been punched in the face while out in Kings Cross.

During the off-season I had been overcome by a sense of my own grandeur. They warn you about it—the second-year blues and the premiership hangovers—but time and time again we look down at the water below and want to soar higher and higher.

After finishing my end-of-year review meeting, where John Blakey had said he thought I was the best crumbing forward in the game, and Horse had added that I was one of the players whose futures he was most excited about, I caught a plane to Bali with a group of teammates. For a week straight I'd sucked down bottles of Smirnoff Ice by the boxload while sitting poolside of a lavish villa. I'd danced on stage at Engine Room and pushed my way to the epicentre of Sky Garden with a menthol cigarette in my mouth.

When I got back to Australia I spent every Friday night at the Hillside Hotel in Castle Hill, paying for the drinks of my friends and buying twenty shots for anyone who could reach the front of the bar. I swiped my bank card without thought. The bartender who I usually ordered from had coached me in high school rugby and each week after a few drinks I'd pester him.

'Hey!' I'd scream out, drunk, obnoxious, unprovoked. 'You're the reason I play AFL. I hated rugby!'

He'd smirk and laugh and ask what I wanted to drink, until one night when he snapped. 'Mate, are you going to tell that fucking story every time you come here?'

Later that night I challenged Olympic hurdler Michelle Jenneke to a race in the car park. She politely declined.

I would get in arguments with bouncers at the drop of a hat and had two or three nights of sheer self-indulgent mayhem. One night I drunk-drove and then narrowly escaped the death-grip lunge of an older man who wanted to tear me limb from limb after I'd thrown tomatoes at his house in the early hours of the morning. Another night ended with a woman who was in the year below me at school and her father carrying me across the front yard and into my house after they had driven past and seen me passed out in the gutter outside Showground McDonald's. The following morning I sent her a bouquet of flowers with a card that said, 'Sorry—from the drunkest guy at Hillside.'

I had signed a two-year contract extension on the day it broke that Lance Franklin was joining the club. I was in Horse's office with Kieren, and we all joked about us going down and telling the media that had started to gather outside about how excited the club was to announce a new signing.

'Yeah, obviously there's been a lot of talk about a big name signing here,' Horse would say. 'Someone we really see as the future of this footy club.' And then I would walk out and say I would take questions.

One morning I awoke from a night of drinking and saw that $16,000 had been deposited into my bank account from the Swans. I had clothing companies sending me free clothes, people messaging me online saying I was their favourite player, and when friends from school bumped into me they would ask in wonderment, 'What's it like, being a professional athlete?' I was nineteen years old, and the world moved around me.

At least, I thought it did.

In that spirit, I went to Liam's house for a drink two nights before pre-season training was set to start.

Liam had moved into a three-bedroom house in Eastlakes with Xavier Richards, around the corner from his old place. The third room was filled by Tom Derickx for a week or two, then by a med student named May.

They scouted the house themselves, but were still a part of the Swans Housing program, I think. Bedrooms in the Housing program were superbly fitted-out on account of the $5000 moving allowance that each player got to spend when they first arrived at the club. Usually that would end up getting you a queen-size bed, a 50-inch TV, a cabinet for that TV, and a PlayStation. Everyone had a PlayStation.

In Liam's living room there was a beer pong table that he and Andrejs Everitt had built, propped up by plastic milk crates. It had artificial grass on top and a metal sink in the middle. At either end, ten circular holes were cut in pyramid formation. The pong table was a regular fixture at house parties in Lismore Street where Shane Biggs would usually DJ using his collection of burnt CDs. There was a lot of early Calvin Harris played, and a Friend Within Remix of 'Renegade Master' by Wildchild would always feature in his post-game boiler room set.

Liam was hesitant to drink with me that night. He had injured himself the season before and was bent on proving something the coming football year. As was I, but I guess I thought it would come easier to me than Liam did for himself. Still, I persuaded him to play a few games of beer pong with me. The cups were filled past the first line with vodka, and topped with lemonade. I lost all three games.

'Alright,' I said after forcing the last drink down my throat. 'Let's head out.'

Liam, without much of a say, put on his jeans and I ordered an Uber. While we waited for it to arrive, I told Liam he had a rubber arm. Easily twisted.

Our local haunt was World Bar. I'd become friends with a guy named Jordy who worked the door. He was a Swans fan, and told me to message him whenever we wanted to come by.

He'd pass us a handful of drink cards and push us through to the front, past everyone else who had to wait.

There were three levels inside, each catering to a different musical taste and agenda. Whenever we went, we'd inhabit the bottom floor, which we called The Dungeon. It was a dimly lit sweatbox of bodies jostling to heavy EDM. There was a DJ booth with VIP seats behind it at the front of the dance floor, and you could order teapots from the bar beside it.

The corridors stemming from the entry way were narrow; it wasn't uncommon to bump people as you walked by. On this night I walked through the door to the left, heading towards The Dungeon. I turned around to ask Liam what he wanted to drink. When I did I saw a guy pushing him. The guy was my height, so much shorter than Liam. He was erratic in his movement, trying to rip Liam's shirt off him. Liam, with his longer arms, pushed the guy well away and walked off, back through the doorway towards a bar in the opposite room.

I don't know why, but I sought to make peace by shaking the guy's hand. I extended my right hand out towards his and said, 'We're all good, aren't we?'

He showed his teeth—in a friendly way, I thought.

I stepped towards him, but when I looked down at my hand, unmet by his, I figured out what was about to happen.

Crack.

Crack.

Two jabs, square to the left-hand side of my upper lip. I felt the impact on my teeth, and then was overcome by an almost euphoric numbness. Like a thousand tiny pins had been simultaneously inserted into my face.

Dazed, I stepped back, and looked into my own eyes which stared back from a mirror on the wall. I could see my loosely hanging upper lip and a stream of blood pouring out and down my chin. I wiped it away with my hand which I then dragged across the painted white walls around me. My bloodied fingers left four fading trails.

People around stared, open-mouthed, in shock. I heard somebody say, 'Jesus Christ, you need help.'

I headed out the front to get in a taxi, but the bouncer took me back in. He ushered everyone out of the room and walked behind the bar, where he crouched to grab a cloth from beneath the bench and douse it in vodka.

'Hold still,' he said.

I winced. 'Do you reckon I need stitches?'

'Yeah.'

'Do you know how to do it?'

He laughed. 'This is the limit of my medical expertise. You need to go to a hospital, brother.'

While a vodka-soaked, bloodied rag was being dabbed against my lip, Liam walked into the room. 'Fuck, you alright?' he asked, standing beside the bouncer.

I moved the rag away from my face. 'Yeah, need stitches though.'

'Yeah, shit. No good.'

I thanked the bouncer and Liam hailed a taxi out the front. We got in the back seat and the driver asked where to.

'Take me to a hospital,' I said.

'St Vincent's is just down the road, that good?'

'No, not there, somewhere else. The one in Randwick. Whatever that one's called. Take me there.'

I was paranoid that a camera crew would be at St Vincent's and that I'd end up on TV.

'Righto,' he said and started the meter.

———

When I finally got to see a doctor it was mid-morning. He said I'd need plastic surgery. While he was applying a dressing to my face he asked what had happened.

'I was punched in the face in Kings Cross,' I said.

He shook his head once and said I was lucky that I only had a split lip.

Liam had stayed with me in the waiting room all night, and after I saw the doctor I told him he didn't have to wait around any more. He asked if I needed anything and I said if he could bring back a phone charger for me that would be great.

I called my parents first. And then Horse.

'Horse . . .' My voice shook. 'I'm alright, but . . . I went out last night and got punched in the face, and I need surgery.'

He was taken aback, but was relieved that I was okay. Like the doctor, he said he thought I was lucky.

They wheeled me in for surgery and I didn't eat solid foods until Tuesday. I arrived day one of pre-season with a string of blue-wire stitches in my face. I must've been asked forty times what had happened.

In the afternoon meeting, Horse stood up the front and asked everyone who had made a statement at training that day. Lloyd Perris raised his hand because he'd come second in the time trial, as did Marshy and Locks who both ran PBs.

'Who else?' Horse said, eyebrows raised, looking at all corners of the room. 'Remember, statements don't always have to be good.'

I know he wasn't directing this at me; one of the boys had sat down on a park bench after running a 12-minute time trial, but still, I sat trying to avoid his gaze with blue wire hanging from my lip.

———

Three months after the night I was hit, I sat in front of the heater at my parents' house with the five o'clock news on in the background. The lead story was about a young man named Daniel Christie who was in a coma. He had grown up in the same area as me and gone to the high school around the corner from my house. We were the same age, and had mutual friends on Facebook. On New Year's Eve, Daniel had been walking down Victoria Street in Kings Cross with his brother when he was struck from behind. He fell, hit his head on the road and lost consciousness. He was taken to St Vincent's Hospital, and two days later the Christie family turned off his life support. I don't include this story to liken our situations. I just wish I could tell you that this moment made me aware of my own mortality—but the truth is, it didn't. Something within me had been increasingly geared towards a denial of that mortality, and to this day I still feel it buffering the truth of my own transience. However, not as strongly as it once did.

CHASE, TACKLE, SPREAD

Journal entries from 2014

February 12th

Intraclub today. I am a game changer. I am a fierce competitor. I am never beat in a 1-on-1. I am an aggressive tackler. I cannot be defended with my speed and agility. I am the best front-and-square player in the competition. I kick goals.

———

I played alright. Fox Sports had me as B.O.G. [Best on Ground]. I was really clean at ground level, and hit more targets with handballs. Kicked 1 goal + 2 out on the full. Really have to focus, move faster.

February 24th

Extremely pissed off: I only had 3 one-percenters in NAB round 1. That's not me. I am a high-pressure forward. I've done it before—it's a mentality that I have to chase everyone down. I'll get back to a defence-first mentality: 5th off line, pick out sweeper and get to him. Stalk more at stoppages, get to sweeper. Chase down: any time the ball is near you, go for the man with the ball, don't worry about your man, hunt them down.

This week I will have 20 pressures—5 a quarter. I will prove that I am the pressure forward who we need. Each quarter chase someone and tackle aggressively. Tomorrow at training it starts—hunt them down, prove that you can do it.

February 25th
Kicked goal of the year on Lakeside right in front of Sofía Vergara (Gloria from *Modern Family*).

My focus for West Coast: relentless pressure, reaction time, someone gets the ball then go chase. Closer as stalker, get to man at the back, didn't do this in NAB round 1. Lead-up as a forward, be a breaker.

February 27th
CHASE TACKLE SPREAD
CHASE TACKLE SPREAD

We have guys who will kick goals—all I have to do is be the maniac and hunt down the opposition with relentless pressure.

Post-game: had 11 tackles, forward pressure (tick), clean (tick) front and square (tick).

Just lower eyes going inside 50.

March 7th

Last night I kissed Kathryn for the first time. The girl I had a huge crush on all the way through school. At 10.30pm she messaged me and said we should hang out when she finishes work at the casino at 2.30am. So I set my alarm and she came over at like 3. We just laid in bed with the lights off and kept getting closer till I pulled her over and we kissed a few times. She said, 'Now what?' and I didn't know. I walked her outside and said goodbye, but didn't hug her or anything. She was chewing peppermint gum. I can still taste it.

Game tomorrow: I won't get much game time. I just need to do my best in short bursts.
HIGH IMPACT CHASES AND RUNS.
BACK YOURSELF IN.
GO, HUNT THEM DOWN, TACKLE, PRESSURE, CHASE.
Clean at ground level. Composed with ball. Clinical finisher.

March 10th

Playing reserves this week. My focus is on getting back in the first team. I will have 20+ pressures and kick goals. I will be a maniac and hunt down the opposition. I will take them on with my pace. Aggressive. 1-on-1. Dominate. Dominate at training. Show you should play. Pressure.

March 14th

Reserves game vs GWS tomorrow. Playing wing/half-forward. Be confident that you are an AFL player. No one can match your work-rate. Chase. Tackle. Pressure.
GO—TACKLE—CHASE.

YOU ARE ALWAYS ABLE TO GET THERE.
JUST GO.
RUN WITH BALL.
BACK SELF TO KICK GOALS.
I fucking hate GWS.
I will give Horse no option but to pick me.
CHASE, TACKLE HARD, PRESSURE.
Clean, composed, clinical.

March 17th
Reaction to my game: 10 disposals, 11 one-percenters, 3 chases. Created 3 opportunities for goals. I only really played three quarters so if I get my preparation right, I should aim for 15 disposals and 15 one-percenters.

I must only be on for 5–7 mins then get off, am no good after that. You need that burst so you can explode when on.

Instead of handballing, use your legs to get out of the contest. You are quick, strong and agile—no one will tackle you so just go and kick goals, who cares if you get tackled.

Focus for next week: Shorter bursts on field. Use pace out of contest.

You might only get 10 touches, but can have 10 scoreboard impacts.

March 19th
Horse said my reaction time over the past few weeks has been poor. After my debut he said I needed to be cleaner, keep my

eye on the ball, and now that's a real strength of my game. That's the focus. REACTION TIME. Can I influence? Close outlets. Don't spectate. Bang. Go.

March 20th

My GPS was still the best in the twos by a mile.

Must hit 140 strides > 18km/h

20 sprints > 25km/h

HSE [High Speed Efforts]: 1.3/min

Distance over 18km/h > 2000m

Focus at training: Reaction time, always looking for outlet to close or influence. Movement and energy around contest. Always be leading, hooking, making it tough to play on you. Lead hard on short 45s, try and get some marks. Add another string to your bow.

March 21st

Before training, Horse made us all jog to the top of the Valley of Death at Lakeside, then he got us all in a circle and pulled out some boxing gloves and said, 'It's time to sort out some bad blood. Pebbles . . . Buddy . . .' (This was reaction to a news article saying that Pebs was dropped after a fight with Bud.)

Horse: 'Do we need mouthguards?' Buddy: 'Nah, I won't get hit anyway.' Pebs: Grins and laughs. Fight went for 5 seconds.

Trained well, movement to get short 45s and longer leads worked. Aggressive slide also gave me more space.

March 23rd

Awesome day yesterday. Went and watched Rhys at Brazilian jiu jitsu comp—he's really good now. Won his first fight by submission after some tall bald guy had him in guard for 4 mins. Only just lost the second fight after he almost pulled an amazing arm bar. Then I went to Patty Mitchell's (Roosy's house) with Lloyd Perris, Biggsy and Cray. Played old '90s beats then went to The Sheaf.

March 25th

Was great at training today—used my pace to run around opponents and kick goals. Did a great spoil on Xavier Richards, which everyone loved, and was getting to good spots. Aggressive slide helps me lose my opponent. I dictate where we go. More hook leads. Horse said at the Swans Foundation cocktail party, 'If he keeps training the way he did today it won't be long till he plays.'

March 27th

Am playing reserves on the weekend. Ryan O'Keefe selected in forward pocket. To get a game I must dominate. Make them tackle me. Kick goals. Beat my opponent. Chase. Pressure. React first.

April 3rd

Not playing seniors again. It's a challenge that will make me as a player, force them to put me as B.O.G. in the 2s. Stand up in a tough game. Force them to pick me. Clean/pressures. More chase-downs. As you are about to come off, make a chase-down tackle.

April 7th

18 disposals

16 pressures

1 goal 1

2400m > 18km/h

Getting close to tearing it open.

All I have to do is finish.

Take opportunity.

4 goals and 16 pressures would be a great game.

Pressures

Tackle

Chase

Spoils

Intercepts

Blocks

April 8th

I get so pissed off when I read the reserves reports. I never get a mention. It's always Jake Lloyd, Dan Robinson and Shane Biggs. They just get the footy, which is easy in their positions.

I am ahead of where I was last year. I consistently get 15–20 touches and 12+ pressures. To play seniors I must start finishing my goals/assists.

FOCUS:

Clean hands.

Finishing: last one off the track.

Always doing extra kicking.

April 10th

Not even named in 25-man senior squad. Today I draw a line in the sand. I train my arse off tomorrow. Train how I play. Lead to space. React to space. Run and carry. Goals. Win 1-on-1s.

April 12th

Had a good talk with Joey Kennedy. He said I am thought of very highly at the club because you know what you're going to get from me. Says the playing group has a lot of confidence in me. Said he was in a similar position to me at the Hawks— just on the edge. I said I like this challenge because the great players overcome obstacles easily and I want to earn my spot and make sure I'm ready for the call-up. He seemed impressed by my frame of mind. 'Just kick goals,' he said.

April 13th

Frustrating game. Had 13–14 touches vs Queanbeyan. Small ground at Blacktown so the ball was always going over my head. How will today make me better? I must play through the midfield. Talk to Peter during the week about playing in the mids rotation. Learn structures of Josh Francou and become a student of the game.

Was so frustrating. Got to the right spots at least 8 times and guys didn't use me on the overlap run, and another 5 times they didn't kick it to my space. Peter said I would have played better if I was with the seniors because they'd hit me. He also said I'm still ahead of Deano. If I get a chance this week I'll make it count—they won't discredit me due to a one-off game.

Keep working hard. Head down, arse up. Work hard every day.

April 14th

Watched yesterday's senior game as a team. No one getting front and square, no forward pressure. Ball exiting too easy. No one said anything the entire game, then Stuey Maxfield, who was sitting at the back, said, 'What the fuck is going on, why hasn't anyone said anything?' I can be that high-pressure small forward, I can harass defenders and get front and square. I don't go kick chasing and I stick to my role. I can bring another dimension to the team and I'd love to get a crack at Ryan Crowley this week. Watched the semi last year and wanted to jump on the field and hit him. I could've had way more pressures on the weekend. From now on I chase everything, tackle everything. The rest will come. The weekend's game didn't suit me, but I'm ready for seniors.

April 17th

Playing deep with Buddy and LRT. My role is simple: keep the ball inside our 50.

Pressure—chase, tackle, 2nd and 3rd efforts in the 10m circle.

Crumbing—get to good spots, you are the best there is.

React first to slide, lead or get back in. Slide early then close teasing distance.

Effort, body, reactions.

Hit Crowley.

I am the most dangerous and exciting small forward in the competition. My pressure is the best pressure. I chase, tackle and harass.

April 21st

Beat Freo. Played my role well, all coaches happy. 10 pressures, 6 fwd pressures (equal most) and up there in all GPS sprints. And I only played three quarters. My pressure was noticed—in the meeting Shawry said Freo backmen were scared that I was there. I need to keep doing it, the offence will come. If I can get 15 pressures, 10 touches, 1–2 goals a game, I'll be happy.

More pressure by staying switched-on. I missed an easy spoil that could have led to a goal, and did a bump after a chase when I should've tackled. Vince said I have what we'd been lacking. My game is all based on effort and reaction—I can do that every week. Best feeling kicking that goal. Exhilarating.

In the first quarter I hit Crowley at a stoppage inside our forward 50. He went down, the umpire blew a free kick, and when he got the footy he said, 'You're a fucking idiot, mate.' The runner came on and pulled me off the field. I was handed the phone on the bench. *'BJ, AS LONG AS YOUR ARSE POINTS TO THE GROUND YOU'LL NEVER DO THAT SHIT AGAIN AT THIS FOOTY CLUB.'*

'GET IT DONE?'

The Tuesday after the Fremantle game a group of us young players had dinner in Coogee together. A WhatsApp message went out saying to meet at Churrasco—an all-you-can-eat Brazilian restaurant on Coogee Bay Road.

It was forty dollars a head, and we each pulled out a fifty. The youngest counted the money and paid, and then we took the change down to the Coogee Bay Hotel and put it on trackside.

Every time we went to a TAB, someone would tell the story about how Shawry (Rhyce Shaw) had once put $1 on a 12, 11, 10 trifecta on trackside for a hundred straight races, then left, and come back to scan his ticket to see he'd won $30,000, or something like that. I don't like gambling. I don't get a thrill from it, but I'll have a punt if my mates are.

There'd been about ten boys at dinner, but as they slowly left one by one there remained just four of us, surrounded by desperate punters cradling schooners, and Irish backpackers. Someone brought up the idea of going to a Thai massage place that they'd heard of around Bondi Junction.

'We've got tomorrow off yeah, so why not,' he said, the implication being that we'd get *rub 'n' tugs* or *happy endings*. 'What do you reckon?'

In the car on the way we joked about the team meeting on Monday, and took turns offering up impressions of the coaching staff and physios. My contribution was to repeat what Horse had said to me on the phone during the weekend's game after he'd pulled me from the ground for hitting Crowley at a forward-50 stoppage.

'BEEEEJAAAAYYY, AS LONG AS YOUR ARSE POINTS TO THE GROUND YOU'LL NEVER DO THAT SHIT AGAIN AT THIS FOOTY CLUB!'

On Monday Horse had clarified things with me, and we had a laugh about it. I think it helped that we'd won.

In the car this was followed by calls of, 'SPREEEEEAD', 'SHIIITHOUSEEE' and 'GET UP JESSIE! GET UUUUUP!'

Horse is a big brooding man with legs thicker than my torso. Actually, even his calves are thicker than my torso. To imitate his yell, you have to draw bass from the depths of your stomach and force out a restricted boom from the roof of your mouth. It also helps if you tuck your tongue down so that it presses against the backs of your teeth, and round your pursed lips, as if you're letting out the howl of a desert storm. I always found Horse's stature, voice and gameday-coaching-box antics to be quite misleading. He held a gentle care for those around him, which sometimes became harder to see the closer he got to the field. But we were all like that: sufferers of *white line fever*.

We arrived out the front of the Thai massage place and pulled over. One of the guys got out and took a look, and then shook his head to let us know they were closed. To be honest I don't think he really looked that hard.

'So, you boys want to go somewhere else then?'

There was a pause. A communal inward breath of resignation. Then a voice spoke: 'Yeah, sure, I, uh, I know there's a place in Surry Hills we can go to.'

I was silent, sitting in the rear left seat of the car. Silent, with the choice to leave, but wanting to stay.

We parked on a street adjacent to Crown Street.

'It's just in there,' said the guy who'd suggested the place, pointing out the window.

We slammed the car doors shut and walked towards the front entrance. It was dark outside and there was no foot traffic.

Standing on the resident's side of a waist-high steel gate, I saw a security camera over our heads. There was a blue neon light above the door.

Someone knocked. We waited. Doubt crept in.

'Maybe this isn't it.'

The door opened and a woman looked past us with squinted eyes. She then did a quick scan of each of us before stepping to the side and ushering us inside.

'Take a seat, take a seat,' she said, pointing to a brown leather couch. The other three boys sat on the lounge while I stood next to the arm.

It was a nice place. There was a strong smell of lavender coming from the incense that was burning on top of what used to be a fireplace. The smoke rose up past a painting of countryside which was hanging on the wall. The woman who had let us in stood on the other side of a glass-topped coffee table. 'Does anyone want any tea or water?' she asked.

We all shook our heads. I could see the teabags were in boxes next to the incense.

There was a bowl full of singly packaged Mentos resting on the table. I took one and put one end of the packet in my mouth while I pushed down on the other end with my thumb and index finger so that the air inside the packet popped it open and forced the lolly out.

The woman, who I assume was in charge, looked us up and down again. Her hands were clasped together in front of her belly. 'Alright, stay, stay, let me get the girls.'

She walked out of the room and I could hear her instructing people in a language I didn't understand. It had that forceful sound which I think is just the harshness of unfamiliarity.

She returned to the room, smiled in our direction, and then placed herself in the corner of the room opposite the door she had just walked out of.

One by one, women wearing lingerie entered the room and stood on the other side of the coffee table. Some would smile and wave, and say their name, others would press their breasts forward with their arms. One woman wearing bright pink kicked her heel up before disappearing into the black on the other side of the door.

After they had all come through—about seven of them— the woman asked us who we were interested in.

'Can we just have a minute to talk?' said one of the boys.

'Sure, sure,' replied the woman before going back to the desk by the front door.

The conversation was swift. No one wanted to stay.

'Alright, let's head.'

We grabbed more Mentos and walked past the lady at the front. 'Sorry, not for us.'

'Okay, bye, bye, come back soon!'

The door shut and we walked through the gate. 'So, now what?'

We stood in a circle, each of us chewing a fruit-flavoured Mentos. The street was still empty.

'Well,' said one of the boys, looking at all three of us in one swivel of his head. 'I know there's another place not far from here, and then another one right across the road from where we just were. Maybe we should split up and two of us can go there, and the other two can find the other place? Getting four girls at one place is a bit much I reckon.'

'Yep, sounds good,' I said.

'Meet back here when you're done.'

The two others walked up the road and turned the corner, to the right, while me and my partner stood out the front of a terrace with a red light above the door, near where we had just been.

I knocked. Two elderly Asian women stood before me. One put her hand on my back as she directed me towards the couch. The room was set up identically to the place we had just been. They offered us tea and water and on the table opposite the couch was a bowl of Mentos.

The same routine happened. The girls walked out one by one, introducing themselves by saying their name, before walking back out. The whole time I was hoping to see someone who looked familiar, or at least a girl who smiled like someone I knew.

The two women bought a scrapbook over with images of all the girls we had just seen. Me and my mate had a conversation off to the side.

'Which one do you want?' he asked.

'I . . . I like this one. What about you?'

'The older bird? Right, that works. I want this young thin one, she's pretty fit.'

We pointed to the women we had chosen in the scrapbook, and then one of the elderly women walked out of the room while the other stood with us and asked us how long we wanted. Thirty minutes cost $180. There was an ATM machine behind us. I took the money out and then the girl I had pointed to in the scrapbook re-entered the room, grabbed my hand and took me upstairs.

In the room, the decorations on the ceiling were Victorian. The sheets on the bed: floral.

In the far corner was a shower with no screen or curtain around it. Just a flat, rounded steel head facing a square section of tiles which broke up the wooden floor.

The woman passed me a towel and a single piece of circular soap wrapped in a plastic that felt like tissue paper.

'Okay, have a shower, sweetheart,' she said. 'And what's your name?'

'Brandon,' I said, realising that it was just me and her in the room, and that just a few minutes before this we had been complete strangers.

I turned the taps on and took off all my clothes while she opened the bedside table and rummaged around for something. I then ripped off the adhesive patch from my stomach which fed insulin into my body—something I used to do before sleeping with any woman.

I faced away from her and covered myself with my hands for a second before I realised how ridiculous it was to be doing that considering what was about to happen. I pulled my hands away and started to use the soap.

'Make sure you wash all over,' she said. Then she joined me and took the soap and started rubbing it against my skin.

It was first time I'd ever showered with a woman.

She turned off the taps and we dried ourselves and then she pushed me onto the bed. While I lay there, she set a timer, which sat beneath a lamp upheld by a curved wooden leg, for thirty minutes. I could hear it ticking down.

She put her body on top of mine and kissed my neck before moving her head down. I could see the place where her black hair parted. She must've been about forty years old.

She started biting my chest and I tensed up and pulled away.

'Uh, I don't like that,' I said.

'Okay, no worries, sweetheart.'

She stopped biting, and we had sex.

———

The timer went off and the woman stopped. Her demeanour changed. The past half-an-hour had been an act, and I understood that. This was her job.

She stood up and asked if I was on drugs, because I hadn't finished.

'Nah,' I said, 'I'm . . . I'm sorry about that, it's—'

'It's fine,' she said.

While putting my clothes back on I asked for her name, but she mustn't've heard me because she didn't respond.

When I walked out of the room a man came out of the next doorway with a briefcase in his hand and suit jacket over his arm. I pushed myself against the wall so he could walk past. He didn't look at me.

My friend was waiting for me downstairs, sitting on the couch. I took another handful of Mentos from the bowl on the table and we left.

As we walked outside the two elderly women called out, 'Come back soon!' Neither of us replied.

We waited by the car and saw the other two guys walking down the road.

'You boys get it done?' one said.

'Yeah, you?' one of us said.

'Yeah.'

They were also chewing Mentos. We got in the car and they dropped me home.

One of the other guys said that the place he had gone to just had a mattress on the floor in a room.

I went into the footy club at nine the next morning and did a goalkicking session with Nick Davis. We worked on a new set-shot routine where I'd take six walking steps and then four-to-six jogging steps before kicking. My focus was on keeping a straight line to the centre of the goals and trying to land the ball on a spot where the goal umpire's head would be, so that I didn't over-kick it and risk pulling the kick to the right. After about fifty shots we moved on to snaps. From the left-hand pocket I kicked with my right foot off one or two steps, figuring that was a good routine.

KINTSUGI

Kintsugi [noun]: The Japanese art of repairing broken pottery with gold—the idea being that by embracing imperfection, something more beautiful is created.

Journal entries from 2014

April 24th

Dropped. Fucking shattered. Replaced by Goodesy and Jake Lloyd because the coaches are concerned that if there's an injury they will have to rotate Goodesy highly and Lloydy is a better runner than me. I'm fucking filthy. I played my role; I deserve to play. Fuck them, fuck them all—if they want to treat me like this I'll make them look stupid. My next game I'll play with aggression at every contest. I GET THE BALL AND I PRESSURE. Play half-forward, wing and mid.

I hope the senior team loses on the weekend; I hope we have shit forward pressure. I've never been so pissed. Fuck them.

April 27th

Worst weekend to be travelling emergency. Seniors won a shitty game vs Melbourne and the reserves won against Brisbane and got on the piss hard. It's all about actions for me. Train well, just relax, your best performances are when you are relaxed. When you kicked 4 against Melbourne you were only expecting to play one quarter and so you put no pressure on yourself.

Look to get involved at every contest. You are an impact player—you might only get 10 touches but you could kick 2 goals and have 5 tackles.

My strengths: forward-50 tackles/chases/pressures, score involvements.

Always look to hook-lead and spread—build your game around speed and spread. No one can stop your 50m sprints. Lead then crumb. Lead then crumb.

April 28th

Training focus tomorrow: spread hard. When we get it, sprint to space where the ball will go.

You are smart and fast, so go as hard as you can for 50–70m to where the ball will go.

Movement in and out of short 45s. Work hard to get goal-side then lead to space. Go as hard as you can.

May 8th

I am now a midfielder with the ability to play forward and kick goals. I'll be around stoppages a lot more, so I'll have more opportunity to get the footy. I'll get pressures through tackles and chases around stoppages.

I'll spread hard from sweeper or point. If you can impact, go. Play with risk and back yourself in.

Wingers: sweep or point. They sit out so let them have that. Go inside and win it.

May 10th

We beat the Giants. Had 5 touches to half-time then played on the wing the whole second half and had another 16. Was really vocal at stoppages, which coaches and Ryan O'Keefe said was good. They said that me going into the middle helped change the game—it gave us more balance and pace. I was really good in scrambles.

I evolved in two ways. Showed I can play mid and get the footy. And showed I can work my way into a game after a slow start.

Went out with Lloyd Perris, Shane Biggs, Patrick Mitchell, Jake Lloyd and Harrison Marsh. Free entry and drinks at World Bar. Went to Hanners' house. Then took Belle (from uni) and her mate to Paul Roos' investment house where Patty Mitchell is living. Broke in the back door. The alarm went off and Roosy called the house.

May 20th

Angry and frustrated. I feel like I'm letting myself down. I haven't been able to play consistent footy. That's not the way it is. I've been in and out due to some unlucky circumstances. Replaced by Goodes, Franklin and McGlynn all coming back from injury. Lloydy and Cunno are getting games because they can play midfield. Okay, well now I respond and play midfield. If I get 25 touches and 15 pressures in reserves they won't hold me out. That's what I will do. I'm excited for this challenge. At the end of the year I will earn more respect from everyone by playing consistent impressive footy for the rest of the year.

Be confident in yourself—you are getting better every day. Play without fear, take risks. You have nothing to lose and everything to gain. Take guys on at training.

Work hard, it'll come.

May 25th

Trained well, 'don't think, do'. Won a few one-on-ones, and looked good when I used my jump to mark/tap. Did some pretty special plays, stepped 3 guys and set up Toby, tap down to Deano, then took a one-handed mark back with the flight. Keep stepping guys. But just give the easy one if it's on, or sprint.

May 29th

Seniors beat Geelong by 110 points. My season starts again tomorrow. All the shit I've been through I push to the side and start afresh. Win my one-on-ones, defensive pressure, spread and work rate. Be selfish and kick goals. Pressure and goals.

As a forward, work with Members and Deano, and make sure you get the ball when it comes your way. Hard effort to get the ball. React first, sprint. See ball, get ball.

My mentality/how I feel? Fuck them. Force them to pick you.

Spread/work rate. Hard. Clean. Run.

No more spectating. Get to as many contests as possible.

May 30th
Tomorrow: get involved.

Demand the ball.

Spread, work rate, effort.

Chase/tackle.

Demand hands.

Be selfish at times, run and carry.

Tomorrow is an opportunity to have fun, to play footy, and to feel good about myself.

Don't wait—go and get the ball if it's not coming to you. Don't hold out once it's in the scramble—get involved to lose your opponent. Start in the structure, then get involved.

Get the footy.

Work with other forwards. Follow Tommy Mitchell to get to footy.

June 5th

Feeling good. Finally played a solid reserves game on the weekend and proved myself to a lot of people who may not have been certain about me. I have the ability to play inside and use my pace around the stoppage. I'm the best loose-ball gatherer.

28 disposals [25 to 3/4-time]
9 one-percenters
3 goals
15.5km run [top by 1km]

Next week we improve again. Practise being hit by ruck. If you ever get in one-on-one with one guy between you and the goals run around them or chip-and-chase. Just back yourself. Be loud at training.

June 6th

This weekend:
Effort, energy, work rate, offensive spread, offensive pressure
Effort, energy, work rate, offensive spread, offensive pressure
Effort, energy, work rate, offensive spread, offensive pressure
Effort, energy, work rate, offensive spread, offensive pressure
Effort, energy, work rate, offensive spread, offensive pressure

Pace around contest, roll out
Pace around contest, roll out
Pace around contest, roll out

Use legs, kick, kick goals. Run both ways. Run both ways. Effort. Energy.

Sweeper: force your man into stoppage to give yourself space.
Post: hold and meet bodies on the way through.
Outside: call a number for an inside hit, chest hit [nudge man under ball, tell insiders to search for you].

Effort energy chase tackle pressure.
Offensive spread, defensive pressure.

What does it look like? Hard, clean, running with ball, goals, tackles.

June 9th
Weekend reserves game vs Gold Coast. In for three quarters (emergency for seniors so came off).
27 disposals [game high = 31]
11 one-percenters [game high = 13]
5 chases
4 tackles

Positives:
Movement around scramble
Clean handballs
Spread
Pressure

Improvement:
Closing outlets
Forward-50 kicks [do work with leading forwards]

June 10th
Things to work on:
Don't over-commit at sweeper, stay outside
Read cues, e.g. dead side
Effort, don't slack off, close outlets

Spoke to Horse—he said he is very excited at my midfield play, can't wait to see me play there more and is excited to see where I will be at next year.

June 11th
Playing seniors this week at this stage. Nothing changes from the past two weeks. I'll get more of the ball because I'll play through the wings. My strength is reacting to inside scramble—our midfield will get me the ball. When forward I chase, tackle, and harass. Have 20+ one-percenters. How? Chase everything.

No one will stop you if you sprint. Step opponents, then go to get a few extra metres, change direction if you don't get used so at least you are where the ball is and you can crumb and scramble.

Ball in scramble? Impact it.

Energy, effort, chase, tackle, pressure, go, offensive spread, defensive pressure.

June 12th
Chase, tackle, pressure, go, energy, effort.

#21 Polec: fucks off forward
#24 Impey
#5 Broadbent
#29 Pittard: left foot
#36 Hombsch
#42 Jonas

Feeling ready, attack ball, chase and pressure.

18 vs 18 at training today: kicked 2 goals, had 4 pressures.

Me or 7th [spare forward] follow in their dangerous half-back (Ebert, Cornes, Polec). Follow them to the stoppage, then hand over.

At forward-50 stoppages: horseshoe/stalker. At 3/4 ground: F1.

June 13th
Energy, effort, chase, tackle, pressure, go
Offensive spread, defensive pressure
Energy, effort, chase, tackle, pressure, go
Energy, effort, chase, tackle, pressure, go
Energy, effort, chase, tackle, pressure, go
Offensive spread, defensive pressure
Offensive spread, defensive pressure

Tomorrow will be one of the best experiences of my life. I get to play in the best team surrounded by absolute guns. They will help me and pull me to their level. Nothing changes in how I play. If the ball is there to be won, I get it. Crack in.

Get involved in scramble, front and squares, and get to every forward-line crumb. I'll have confidence on the wings, and opportunities to get the footy.

#1 Boak
#5 Broadbent
#7 Ebert
#8 Hartlett
#9 Gray
#18 Cornes
#24 Impey
#29 Pittard
#36 Hombsch
#42 Jonas

Watch their spread. Vocal in structures, talk to guys around you. Contest by contest. Kick goals.

June 14th
Kieren's 150th. We beat Port Adelaide who were two wins clear on top of the ladder. Thought I played well, provided good pressure and some drive forward.

To improve: Back yourself more, run around blokes and kick goals. Start running around. I did it once tonight, and I can do it more.

June 17th
Focus tomorrow on offence. I feel that I get all the defensive stuff now like second nature. Now I can attack. I had the

opportunity to get probably 15–16 disposals in three quarters against the best defensive team in the competition. All I had to do was hunt the ball, demand it more off guys. We want the ball in your hands. Close to two front-and-squares: attack footy + 2. Close to 2 in scramble + 2. Demand more = + 4. Demand ball. Get into scramble. Then push hard forward.

June 23rd
Positives:
17 disposals
11 one-percenters
Clean
Created opportunities
Clear shots @ goal [2 others I could've tried]
Got to contest, didn't fear my opponent
Spread hard
Overhead marking

Improvements:
Finishing goals (practise quick kicks from 20m out and 50m out)

Keep doing:
Spread hard to space, break early
Getting in hard
Stalking timing has been good
Getting to scramble, back yourself to win footy or react first to get man

Effort, energy, chase, tackle, pressure, go, offensive spread, defensive pressure.

June 27th
Energy, effort

June 29th
Frustrated at the sub rule. It's so annoying, I was dangerous so many times when I came on but guys wouldn't use me. 2 × marks inside 50. 2 × front-and-squares. Focus on work-rate. On getting to contest. On winning ball, getting inside 50 hard.

June 30th
This is my story, no one else's. I will get to the top. It's not where you start, it's where you end up. This time right now is vital in instilling in me a deep hunger that cannot be taught. This process is making me the hungriest player in the comp. My fear? Not being part of the Grand Final this year.

Game plan: win inside or spread.
Practise that hard spread.
Do 5–10 leads with Rampe after training.
Work on getting ball: fitness + patterns.

July 8th
65% game time (three quarters) in seniors.
15 one-percenters, 12 disposals, 3 shots @ goal.
I'm so close to becoming that player.

Horse said I'm probably too hard on myself, but that drive is how I get better all the time—it is something that the great players have. He says they're very happy with my progress, that I had a few 'tough cunt plays'. Respect was earned.

July 17th

I am the most driven and hardworking player. My work-rate and attitude will get me to where I belong: on top. It may not happen this year—some things are out of my control—but I'll get there. Stay the course. Repeated efforts, day in, day out. Macca missed out on playing in the premiership his second year. Stay hungry. Play seniors: keep going. Reserves: midfield, win ball, big numbers.

Weekend in the seniors: provided a bit when on, good spread, got involved. 17 mins, 5 touches.

July 24th

Dropped. Again. Deano playing instead because they feel if Tippo goes down early they can leave him on there to run. I'm fucking angry. I'll use this to motivate me—I have a hunger and desire that no one else does. Aaron Rodgers [Green Bay Packers QB] kept college rejection letters to motivate him— he said he had a drive that someone who didn't have that rejection wouldn't have. When I get my chance, I'll never let it go.

July 27th

Michael Jordan didn't make his high school basketball team because he was too short. Instead they selected his 6ft6 friend. Michael was clearly more talented, but this was out of his control.

30 min slider number 3 = 3.19km

Focus:
Run around guys
Play in midfield
Attack ball OR Stay inside

Looking forward to playing a game this week.

July 28th
Really good talk to Horse. Said he knows I'm frustrated—
he had the same talk with Parks two years ago about being
sub and in and out of the team. Just focus on what I can
control.

Big areas for improvement: skills (finishing) and conditioning.

Horse says it's important for me to play games coming into
finals. If I play reserves it'll be a full game in the middle = good
opportunity to get possessions.

He really likes my midfield stuff. I need to do it more before
I play mids at seniors, that's why Lloydy got games because he
played mid in reserves for two years.

Horse sees me being in midfield next year.

My focus:
Skills
Finishing
Hard inside

Test yourself in 18 vs 18 at training.
Go over hits with mids/ruck.
Talk to Joey re: midfield set-up.

September 5th
Lloydy only works one half of the ground and relies on outlets.
Doesn't chase ball, knows when he's not a chance.

October 4th
So I decided not to go to Thailand tomorrow. I feel my ankle
is not as strong as it could be and if I want to be on track for
a big pre-season I need to get it right. I want to make a huge
impression when I come back.

'The best pace is a suicide pace, and today's a good day to die.'
—Steve Prefontaine

I've written my training program, now it's about action. About
loving the pain of not being able to go, but then finding a way.
That's my ecstasy.

'NO'

Towards the back-end of the 2014 season I rolled my ankle in a reserves game on the SCG.

I'd never really been injured before. While most of my teammates were arriving to the beach on Sunday mornings battered and bruised, wrapped in Tubigrip, and were checking in to injury clinics first thing on Monday mornings, I had, with the exception of the week before my debut, never had even the slightest twinge. The physios and conditioning staff would often joke about their lack of interaction with me.

So when I rolled my ankle it was a new experience. The adrenaline numbed the pain, and I played the whole second half on it. When I took my boot off it was swollen and bruised, a mix of purple, green, blue and brown. I spent the rest of the night with my foot intermittently submerged in a bucket of ice—twenty minutes in, twenty minutes out—watching *Dexter* in the spare room at Kieren's.

The next morning I went to the club to use one of the Ice 'n' Easy machines, which are like high-tech ice buckets on steroids. We were meant to be at the beach as a team, but I texted Spurrsy and said my ankle was no good, and he told me to go into the club and rehab on my own.

There was a rugby league game on at the Sydney Football Stadium, so I couldn't park out the front on Driver Avenue, which meant I had to limp about three hundred metres from Fox Studios. With every step I fought off the idea that this would be the end of my season.

When I arrived at the club I took the elevator to level one and dug the plastic scoop into the crushed-ice machine, which sat in the corner of the physio room next to the NormaTec pants, and started shovelling tiny avalanches of ice into the plastic casing of the machine. I then strapped the velcro padding around my ankle and pressed some buttons on the dashboard and watched as water flowed through the tubes to fill the wrap around my ankle. I thought I was alone, and had my eyes fixed on the TV, watching ESPN, while I lay one of the massage tables. Then a teammate came up and asked what had happened.

'Fucked my ankle just before half-time,' I said.

'Ah shit, did you come off?'

'Nah, we had no one on the bench so I stayed on.'

'They'll like that,' he said, raising his eyebrows and nodding his head.

———

The scans showed it was syndesmosis.

I'd played in seven senior games to that point in the year, which meant I thought that I was in the mix coming into finals.

139

Seniors were on a rampant winning streak which ended up lasting fourteen games. Bud was kicking bags every week, our midfield of Hanners, Joey, Kizza and Parks was the best in the competition, and Mal and Smooch were in the All-Australian conversation.

I didn't want to miss out on my chance, so every day I lied to the physios about the level of pain I was in.

Before our main sessions we had to fill out our markers, which were the results of a series of stretches and jumps that showed how stiff and sore you were. One of the tests was to stand with your foot on a piece of tape that was stuck to the floor and bend your knee, without lifting your heel, till it touched the wall in front of you. When I tried the test I couldn't get any score without lifting the back of my heel because of the excruciating pain the movement caused. So I would lie and say that my right was the same as it had always been.

Another test was the vertical leap, which is where you'd stand on a rubber mat on the floor, put your hands on your waist, and jump up as high as you could while keeping your legs extended straight in the air. When you landed, the digital display would tell you how high you had gone and you'd enter that into the computers. The impact coming back down was too much for my ankle, so again, I never did it. I just put 34 and 32 in every time, which is what my baseline had been since I arrived at the club.

Then when I filled out my wellness—a questionnaire we did at the end of each day where we rated the intensity of training out of ten and evaluated how our bodies felt—there was a specific question that asked if I felt any pain in my ankles, and I always ticked 'no'.

I was doing what I thought I had to do to stay in the mix.

When you're not cemented in the team you don't have that luxury of knowing that at full fitness your spot will still be there, so you grit your teeth and hope that you don't fall down the pecking order. And at the end of the day, being a footballer is largely about managing weaknesses. You are essentially a commodity—a piece of machinery that a club invests in so that you can return victories for the team and revenue for the club. You form personal relationships along the way, but you aren't given a contract, or selected for games, because you're liked.

With my injury I was able to get through games and training by taping my ankle to the point that it couldn't move. My foot felt heavy in my boot. I'd started putting a horseshoe foam pad around my ankle, wrapping it, getting a heel lock and putting more wrap over the top of that again. The thickness was closer to that of plaster; it was very much like a boxer's fist being taped shut and shoved into their mitt. I had to put wet newspaper in my boots for a couple of nights to stretch them out so that my wrapped foot would fit in. Even then, I would often come off the track with purple toes.

I knew things weren't right when we played the Gold Coast Suns out at Blacktown. I lined up on Karmichael Hunt at the front of stoppages and couldn't spread from the contest. Instead of being a transition player who relied on running into open space, I played in the congestion and had to rely on the inside part of my game. I was an outsider trying to be a bull in a box.

It was difficult, because at the time my speed was the thing that could've got me a game. The spot I was gunning for was taken by Jake Lloyd and Harry Cunningham, who were both playing as high half-forward breakers. Their role was to start on one side of the field and then break to the open side when our defence won the ball back and be there for the outlet kick. Every week their running efforts were recognised in team meetings. After the clip Horse would ask, 'How does that make you feel when you look up, defenders?' and someone would reply, 'Fucking really good, takes so much pressure off.'

I ended up playing in the infamous reserves Grand Final up at Aspley. I was initially ruled out of the game, but pleaded my case to the physios again. With their approval, I came into the side for my best mate at the time, Matt Dick. I felt bad about it because I wasn't really right to play, and I think his parents had flown up for the game, which would've been his last for the club as he was delisted a few weeks later after only two years on the list. But my name magnet was above his on a whiteboard somewhere, which meant I was a priority in the club's eyes.

As an aside, that 2014 Grand Final team was probably the greatest reserves team I've ever seen on paper. Tom Mitchell, Toby Nankervis, Shane Biggs, Zak Jones, Tim Membrey, Isaac Heeney (top-up), Callum Mills (top-up), Daniel Robinson, Dean Towers, Xavier Richards, Tommy Walsh, Harry Marsh, Sam Naismith, Ryan O'Keefe and Michael Dickson (top-up) who now punts for the Seattle Seahawks in the NFL. The skeleton of that team spread itself among many other AFL football senior teams, with a Brownlow medal and multiple premierships on its résumé. Still, we lost the game after the siren of a 38-minute final quarter. The game was at Aspley's home ground, and they'd come back from thirty points down in that final quarter, so they probably deserved to win if I'm being honest—though there was an undeniable suspicion about the length of the quarter, and the siren going with the ball in their hands having a shot at goal. The ironic or heart-breaking thing—depending on how you look at it—is that in our pre-game meeting Lloyd Perris identified the player who kicked that goal as the 'heartbeat' of their team. 'If he's up and about,' he said, 'they'll win.'

Me and Xavier Richards walked off the ground during the presentation.

'What a fucking joke,' I said.

Xav said something similar.

It was Pebs' final game for the club; he and Peter cried in the sheds after the game. The memory of this loss comes up a lot for the boys who played that day. Recently I had a drink with Deano and he told me he cried when he saw his parents after the game. If we'd have won then it would've been a joke, but to lose stung deeply. Such was the no-win nature of the reserves.

When we got back to Sydney, I sat down with the physios who said it was best for my career in the long term if I stopped running and focused on getting my body right for the upcoming off-season.

'But I'm still a chance,' I said to Matty Cameron, our head physio.

He just looked at me and shook his head. 'Take a week off and refresh, and then you can start doing off-legs and weights after that.'

Straight after the meeting I walked downstairs and took a water bottle to the dungeon then did a thirty-minute grinder.

I locked myself in the dungeon and weights room for the remaining weeks of the season. When main training was on outside I would do a double off-legs, then come out and do touch with the other rehabbers, before heading up and doing weights with Lloyd Perris who was mainly doing upper body sessions called 'rebuilding the engine' after coming back from an ACL injury he'd sustained during the year. Sometimes we'd do the 'deck of death,' which was where we'd work our way through a deck of playing cards with each suit being assigned to an exercise (chin-ups, medball push-ups, bicep curls, bench, etc.) and the number you pulled represented the reps of that exercise. Face cards were usually assigned to niche exercises— for instance, a king might be two forearm pulls where you'd stand on the bench and twist a thick piece of PVC pipe with straightened arms until a weight dangling from the other end reached your eye line, then lower it back down slowly.

I kept a record of everything I did and had a simple rule of going a little further every time. A little further on the grinder. A little further on the slider. A few more reps on the bench. A little further. A few more. A bit heavier. Each day I set out to be a fitter, stronger, and—as I saw it then—better version of myself. I watched on as our senior team was dismantled by Hawthorn in the Grand Final. I had cancelled my plans to go on the end-of-year footy trip to Thailand so that I could keep training. I didn't get my money refunded, but it was a sacrifice that proved where my priorities where. As my teammates flew out, I was in the dungeon doing a grinder, telling myself that all the pain would be worth it.

KNUCKLES

Every football club tries to con itself into thinking that they work harder than everyone else. So I write these next few words with both conviction and a grin: there was a culture at the Swans around hard work that I'm confident was unmatched in the competition.

When guys from other clubs joined our list, they'd always remark on how tough our pre-season sessions were, and we'd take pride in that. Within the playing group, there was this bloodthirsty hunger and drive that to an outsider would border on bullying, such was the intensity with which things were demanded from you. But as insiders, we liked how stoic we could be as we repeatedly told ourselves that we were hard on each other because we wanted to get better, and because we cared.

In one of my first weeks at the club I was shown a series of clips from the 2012 Grand Final. I had watched this game from the grandstand in real time, yet the way the efforts were deconstructed inside the four walls of the club made me feel like I had watched a different game.

When people—footy fans, the media—talk about the key moments late in this particular game, a game widely heralded as one of the greatest grand finals of the modern era, they'll mention Kieren's goal, Adam Goodes' dribble from a tight angle, and Mal's snap to seal the game—but none of these highlights featured in our sessions.

The clip that was shown time and time again was Marty Mattner's tackle on the wing.

Ryan O'Keefe kicked the ball into an empty Swans forward 50 with just under two minutes to go in the fourth quarter. The score was Hawthorn 81, Sydney 85. The next team to kick a goal would most likely win.

Hawthorn's Shane Savage marked the ball and played on immediately towards the open side. He kicked the ball long to the space in front of Grant Birchall who was five metres ahead of Marty—or Moose, as we called him. If Birchall took the ball and kicked it forward, Hawthorn would've been a little more than a kick away from goal.

Moose dug in to get over to where the ball was and he made the tackle. Then when he picked up the loose ball, he did something that a lot of footballers wouldn't think to do. Rather than running into the field of play to get a kick, or handballing it away for a cheap stat, he deliberately stepped towards the boundary line and absorbed the tackle from Birchall. By doing this he created a boundary stoppage, which gave everyone time to reset. Had he blazed away and kicked the ball it would've gone straight to Hawthorn players in an uncongested setting and they would've been on the attack again.

From the ensuing stoppage, Mike Pyke soccered the ball forward to Jetts. Jetts had a shot at a goal, which fell short. There was a scramble. A stoppage. Hanners took the ball and rolled out to Mal who kicked the goal that sealed the game. If you ever see the close-up shot of Mal being carried by Ted in the air straight after this goal, look out for Nick Smith screaming to get a spare defender back at the next centre bounce.

The emphasis placed on this kind of effort reinforced for me that, at the Swans, it was the little things that were really valued. On TV I might've seen Malceski's goal, but in the Learning Centre I saw Mattner's tackle. We didn't care about media highlights packages; we saw that our edge over everyone else was the little things, the ugly or invisible parts of the game that no one else notices.

The most important stats to us were the one-percenters, which were the small acts on the field which don't necessarily count as stats. The AFL kept their own version of them, but ours were done in-house by the coaching staff who jotted them down in their reviews.

Our one-percenters were made up of: tackles, chases, spoils, smothers, blocks, intercepts and 'others'—essentially a physical impact on a player. While not everyone could be a great kick, we could all chase and dive and block. The premise was that to be a Blood—the embodiment of the Swans culture—required no talent; it was an attitude, and that is what the one-percenters measured.

In every review meeting the coaches would put up a slide showing how many of these acts each player had. We were all expected to have at least eight per game; if the team could get more than 200 then history showed that we would be very likely to win that game.

When projected onto the screen the high numbers stood out, but so did the low ones. If there was a two or three next to your name then you'd sink into your chair, knowing that everyone could see your lack of effort; you couldn't say you were a Blood with a lack of effort, and that week you wouldn't have a leg to stand on if questioned.

As a small forward, one-percenters were more important to my game than kicking goals. I knew I was never going to have more than fifteen touches a game in the seniors, but if I could have fifteen one-percenters I'd be able to say I played my role.

In one of my first few reserves games I kicked three goals and had twenty-four touches and was one of the best players on the field. I felt good about my game until I checked the one-percenter sheet which was posted at the entrance of the locker room on Monday. In the box next to my name was a '3'. I was gutted. It was embarrassing. Everyone else would see that. *How do you only have three one-percenters in a whole game?* I thought.

———

Not standing out is a big thing at a footy club. We were very much the prime example of Tall Poppy Syndrome. If you walked into the changeroom with a new haircut, everybody would pick up on it and say, 'shairy' (shit haircut). If you wore a new item of clothing it also wouldn't go unnoticed. Some guys had a photographic memory of the kits everyone else owned and wore, which was useful when buying clothes for themselves, because having the same outfit as someone else would lead to both a photo and the 'Sammy same kits' nickname.

New boots were always picked on at training, especially when worn by someone who had just signed a new contract or played their first game. In the warm-up we'd all cry out, 'Geez, you're doing alright, aren't ya?' or 'Matchies!'

Our warm-ups were a constant sniping of each other. If you'd gone out on a date that weekend then blokes would bring it up, or if you'd said something a bit wry in one of the team meetings—trying to excuse a poor effort—it was repeated back to you. One time Horse slowed down a clip of Deano to show that he had taken a short step going into a contest. In the warm-up that week a few of us screamed out, 'LOOK AT THAT, LOOK AT THAT . . . THAT'S A SHORT STEP!'

At Mad Monday we started a tradition called 'the honesty box' where an anonymous question to anyone else in the team could be written down, posted in the box and then read aloud. After I slept with a teammate's sister, the first question read, 'BJ, have you got something to tell?' Follow-up questions asked whether me and my teammate should do 'chairs'—which was when two chairs were placed opposite each other while everyone else circled around in silence, and you had to have a conversation with the person sitting opposite.

It always got pretty heavy, and someone usually had to step in.

If nothing else, we were the rigorous enforcers of conformity.

When Instagram was first starting to take off, no player would dare post a photo of themselves, and if they did then everyone would comment on the photo, and others would screenshot and edit it and post it in the group WhatsApp chat, which I think was called 'Pussy Cunts' or 'Cloggers' for the reserves players and 'Dengue Fever' for the seniors.

Our creativity with nicknames showed how scrupulously attentive we were, and how badly we wanted to peg each other down. Deano had more nicknames than anyone else I've met. 'Betty Crocker' because he'd baked something for the coaches in his first year. 'Daddy' because he was a mature-age recruit, and also living in a house with young players Shane Biggs (Biggsy) and Sam Naismith (Crayfish) exacerbated his maturity. 'Drill Sergeant' because of his army-style short-back-and-sides haircut and for his tendency to take the reins during footy trips. 'Donny22' because his signature looked like it said 'Donny', and his playing number, which was next to every signature, was 22. 'Shadows' because in 2013 he had posted a photo to Instagram of his shadow with the caption 'This bloke's been following me around all day.' And lastly 'Creanage' because, well, I don't think there's a reason for Creanage. Biggsy came up with it and it just sounded strange— so it stuck.

Another teammate of mine had a string of nicknames even more ridiculous—mainly in that their length tended to defeat the general purpose of a nickname. He was deathly allergic to peanuts, so he became 'Peanut'—the double meaning behind this was his aloofness to the general banter that transpired during his first few months at the club. After he tried to order drinks at a bar for the first time in his life—vodka sodas— and said to the bartender, 'Two alcohols please,' he became 'Two alcohols please'. In a senior team meeting he let out a very high-pitched sneeze, which he immediately followed up with a hurried, 'Sorry, Horse.' As such his nickname became a very high-pitched and childlike sneeze, which we exaggerated, followed by an equally exaggerated recital of 'Sorry, Horse.' The 'Sorry, Horse' really took on a life of its own—guys would exclaim it like screaming toddlers while we ran around the flanks in our warm-up. And while playing golf in Coffs Harbour, this same teammate tried to remove a bee from his ball with his club. In doing so he ended up killing the bee. He then ran over to his golfing partner, Adam Goodes, and said, 'Goodesy . . . I killed a bee.' I'm sure there's a lot of mayo added to the story, but regardless, nicknames cared not for the truth, and they were all tacked onto him, especially when someone needed to call at him in warm-ups. Cut to groups of grown men doing a-skips and lateral bounds screaming, 'Yeah Peanut; Two Alcohols Please; AHHH-CHOOO . . . SAWRRY HORSE; Goodesy . . . I killed a bee!'

Not having a nickname at a footy club must be a terrible thing. It'd be as though you don't exist.

But it's a strange thing to want to belong by being cut down.

———

If the leaders felt like our standards were starting to slip, then often they would discuss it and subsequently send out a group message from the club's phone instructing all players to meet at Maroubra Beach at 5am the following morning. We'd all exchange texts and remind each other to set alarms and joke about the idea of deliberately crashing our cars into a streetlight if we knew we were going to be late.

We'd arrive at Maroubra and stay in our cars with the heaters on till 4.59am because the mornings were usually freezing cold come winter. When one person bit the bullet and got out, we'd all make our way over with footy shorts on and towels around our necks. Eyes riddled with sleep would try to make sure everyone was there, you'd look for the number either side of yours—for me, Lewis Jetta and Alex Johnson—and then we'd form a circle on the concrete and get down on our hands and knees for knuckles.

Jarrod McVeigh would usually lead the session, though in an act of sadism, sometimes the player who had caused the session—by missing a massage or something like that—would stand in the middle of the circle and have to make the calls as they watched their teammates suffer for something they alone had done.

A lot of guys doing the knuckle push-ups would stare down at the ground, trying to distract themselves from the pain, but Macca would always keep his head up and stare you in the eyes as he called: *Down. Up. Down. Up. Down. Hold . . . Up. Palms. Knuckles. Palms. Knuckles.*

The push-ups themselves weren't that bad. It was the switching from palms to knuckles and the ten-second holds at the bottom which tore your skin away and left blood on the pavement. There was a trick to using your thumbs to take pressure off your knuckles, but if you got found out then it was another round for everyone.

Knuckles were our staple, but there were also other forms of punishment. One year Jetts had to stand on the beach in Coffs Harbour and tackle five players one after the other who ran at him as hard and fast as they could. I think the order was Kieren, Parks, Joey, Tippo and one other, most likely Zak Jones; it feels like something he would've put his hand up for. Then we got in the water and did the whole *American Sniper* Navy SEAL thing: linking arms while doing sit-ups on the shoreline as waves crashed over our heads.

Punishments weren't just about what had happened—they were an attempt to stop what could happen, to stem the flow of blood coming from the wound of declining standards. Horse used to love talking about on-field mechanisms: 'If one thing fucks up out there, we have mechanisms in place,' he'd always say. We knew that fuck-ups happened in a game, but the likelihood of three or four things in a row going to shit was rare.

———

There is a difference between like and respect; and within the walls of the football club, you'd much rather be respected than liked.

That's what we'd say before doing peer reviews sessions, which were an opportunity to hit someone between the eyes with brutal, uncompromised honesty.

In a peer review the player being assessed would leave the room and fill out a sheet of paper, while the group—broken up into three or four smaller groups—filled out the same sheet.

At the top the player had to write three words to describe themselves as a footballer at that point in time, followed by three words they wanted to be described as. This was usually the Bloods trademark motto: hard, disciplined, united, or simply, *a Blood.*

Beneath there were the headings: Start, Stop, and Keep, under which the player would write about themselves.

'Starts' were usually things like, 'Start doing more extras', 'Start chasing more in games', 'Start being more aggressive on the field', 'Start taking rehab more seriously.' It helped if there were clear, identifiable actions. In one of our development sessions Shane Biggs said to Dan Robinson—who was living with his family in Mosman in his first year and wouldn't hang around much after training—'Start getting around the boys more.' The next year Robbo moved from his lavish family home in Mosman to a worn-down sharehouse around the corner from me in Maroubra.

'Stops' would usually be some inverse of the Starts, but they were the hardest to hear: 'Stop accepting where you're at', 'Stop being quiet on the field', 'Stop letting Tippo beat you in 18 vs 18', and the 'Keeps' were everything that the player was doing right: 'Keep asking for feedback', 'Keep coming in on your day off', 'Keep working on your craft after training.'

We'd usually peer-review two players at a time, one who was doing well and was going to have their tyres pumped, and another who was slipping away and needed to be pulled back in line. Each piece of feedback, though simple, was an invitation to start a conversation, and when two guys started talking to each other everyone else would listen, almost spellbound by the intensity in the room. I've never experienced anything else quite like it. There is a part of me that searches for the same level of honesty in everything I do.

There were a few general rules in a peer review. Use clear and certain language—no maybes, no probablys, no buts to soften the blow. Be as direct as possible, and when you give the feedback you have to address the person, not the room.

'Hey, hey, he's in the room,' Ray would say. 'Talk to him, not us.'

And all feedback had to be followed up on as well. The conversation didn't finish when we left the room.

Right before feedback was given, whoever ran the session—usually Ray McLean or Stuey Maxfield—would say, 'Right, why are we here, why do we give feedback?' To which the response was always, 'To get better' and 'Because we care'. This was to ensure that nothing was taken personally. We were hard, but we were united.

———

I had a red sheet of paper with the Bloods trademark printed on it taped on the back of my locker, as well as on the wall above my bed, and I could still recite it to you word for word today because it became the epicentre of my entire universe during those years. My old diaries are filled with the constant tinkering of my own personal trademark which was a trickle-down of the Bloods mantra. Three words, repeated time and time again, always burning into my brain, telling me who I hoped to be.

However, during my time at the club there were always physical manifestations of drive and determination which impacted me more than the words on the whiteboard.

I sat next to Alex Johnson in the locker room for several years, until he changed to Rhyce Shaw's old number, motivated I feel by that superstition all players have in one form or another, and looking for a fresh start. AJ tore his ACL in a pre-season game out at Blacktown during my first year. His journey since has included seven knee reconstructions in the one leg, with a return to the elite level after five long years of such setbacks. Then, the week after his return he did his other knee for the first time. The seniors were playing Melbourne on the MCG, and the playing group converged on the field after the injury.

'It was silent out there,' one of the boys told me. 'We didn't really want to play after that.'

They went on to win that game, but from what I've gathered it was an almost glacial, numb feeling on the field.

Without playing a game, AJ stayed on the Swans list for five years because he instilled in the team something that no one else could. His nickname was 'The Megaphone' and he was the most competitive human being I've ever met. Even in Wednesday night casual games of *FIFA* he'd stand up and yell in your face and call you a little tip-rat when he scored a goal.

The way he trained, and the way he screamed at you when you were in the room with him, was confronting in its bullish single-minded desire to push further.

'OI, FUCKING GO! FUCKING GO! GOOD BOY! COME ON, FUCKING GOOOO! GOOOOO!'

I can't convey the sheer volume of his voice on the page.

Or if we were playing a handball game outside, usually a game called PEGGY, he'd be screaming out 'P . . . E . . . YOU'RE ON P–E!' and the coaches on the field would have to tell him to shut up.

It doesn't matter how talented you are, young players are notoriously quiet—on the field mainly—and so your voice is something that you need to develop. Alex was the exception to that rule. From day one he was the loudest bloke at the footy club, and every year young players would come in and start to mimic his yell and over-the-top screams while training. By the end of my career I'd come off the field without a voice from the yelling I'd done on the field. It became a goal of mine, to make it to the showers with a half-functioning voice.

Kieren always told me that AJ directed the premiership winning backline as a nineteen-year-old, and that he was going to be captain of the club one day. Had it not been for his injuries then I could've seen that happening, but I guess we will never know. Every time AJ did his knee we'd all be overcome by a sense of despair. Horse would stand up the front of the room and give us an update, and we'd walk out hoping that this time would be different. His journey signified something for us all. Maybe we just didn't want to believe that the game could be that cruel.

I don't know how many doctors and physios told him to stop playing, but I always felt like he was going to go until he couldn't walk anymore.

I haven't spoken to Alex in a while, but last I heard he had been back playing local footy in Victoria till he did his knee again. On social media, it looks like he's busy setting up a cycling business, and that makes me happy to know because it might mean he's found the 'off' switch I think we're all searching for.

426

Four hundred and twenty-six metres.

This is the distance around the inside of the knee-high white fence that encircles McKay Oval in Centennial Park.

Before the 2015 pre-season I bought a trundle wheel from Rebel Sports and walked around the ground not once, but twice, because I wanted to know the exact number.

The first Friday of my second pre-season we had done a session at that oval which I almost couldn't finish. With the temperature in the mid-thirties we did two sets of 300s, 150s and 100s. You could feel the heat reflecting off the short cut grass while we waited for Spurrsy to blow his whistle, and between reps I would put a wet towel on my neck and hope that my legs wouldn't give way.

It was the form of running I was most suited to, but I was no longer content with being one of the best. I now had to be *the* best at this form of running—hence the trundle wheel.

We had eight to ten weeks on our own in the off-season. After having three weeks completely off, we were meant to start with two running sessions a week, and then build up to three by the time the off-season finished.

Once my ankle felt steady I started doing three double sessions a week: one in the morning and one at night.

In the morning I would do the prescribed session, plus an extra 10-minuter as hard as I could to replicate the 3km time trial, and at night, I would do a series of shuttles, sprints and finish with another 10-minuter.

The 3km time trial was the benchmark for fitness in footy at the time (these days it's the 2km). I'd usually be able to sit on the back of Daniel Robinson for the first lap, then every time he would kick when we got our halfway splits and I'd start slowing down as the voice in my head would say things like, *You won't finish if you keep this pace up*, and *You need to slow down*, and *Save it till the end*.

I thought that if I could show I was a good 3km runner then it might make the coaches change their perception of me as a player who could only play forward and who was an interchange liability late in games. But to do that I had to shut this internal voice up, and I thought the best way to do that was to burn myself into the ground with the amount of work that I did.

On the days I wasn't running—Tuesdays, Thursdays, Sundays—I was in the gym doing high-rep circuits, double off-legs and treadmill runs. At the end of each gym session I would see how fast I could do 50 reps of 60kg on the bench press. When I had first arrived at the Swans I could do a maximum of two or three reps of this. Over the summer I went from doing sets of ten to fifteen, to eighteen, to twenty, and by the start of pre-season I was doing twenty-eight reps comfortably, followed by the remaining twenty-two.

Mike, one of the strength and conditioning coaches, joined in with me on a circuit one time. He was a fit guy who competed in triathlons and knew his way around a weights room; he probably had the best rig at the club, players included. I told him to look at the whiteboard to see what I was doing and join in if he wanted. After completing our fourth set of overhead dumbbell shoulder-presses, he let the weights hit the ground and looked at me and said, 'You're a fucking maniac, BJ.'

On Sunday nights I would go to the club on my own and set the treadmill in the warm-up area to 17.5km/h—the time required to run 3km in ten minutes and fifteen seconds—and run until my legs fell out from under me. There was a clip on a string attached to the treadmill that you could clasp to your singlet—an emergency stop measure which would halt the machine if you fell off, which was what happened most times. I liked running on a treadmill—it forces your legs to go beyond your mind, which is something you try to do as a runner, as your mind will usually give up before your body. A treadmill going at a certain pace means you just keep going long after you think you can.

I became so bent on training that I would wake up in the middle of the night to work out. A story about Jake Lloyd's training routine came out towards the end of that year and it drove me deeper. I read it while I was on the way to a game at ANZ Stadium which I was the emergency for. *No one is going to train harder than me*, I thought. So I kept a yoga mat under my bed and woke up at 4am every morning and did one-hundred push-ups and two-hundred sit-ups. It was all about developing a mental edge: knowing that no one else was doing more than me.

As boys started returning to the club before our first official session back, some commented on my new appearance. I was in the showers with Jeremy Laidler after a gym session and he said, 'Jesus, you're in shit nick aren't ya?'

The night before our first session, I asked Charlotte, Kieren's girlfriend—now wife—to shave my head. I was intent on having no distractions in the 3km time trial, and I looked for every avenue to take seconds off my time.

I also wanted my coaches and teammates to think I was a different person. To see me as hard. No, not just as hard. As a fucking relentless cunt.

The following morning I ran a PB and at the end of the week Horse pulled me into his office and said he was impressed with the shape I'd come back in. 'You look like you've got a man's body now,' were his words. He then told me they were thinking about playing a stay-at-home small forward with Tippo and Bud. While stretching on Kieren's floor that night, I pictured playing the role in my head. My heart beat faster and I felt a literal hunger for it.

DILUTE

Hunched over against the wall in the corridor of an apartment block in Coogee with a red plastic bucket stuffed between my limp, bowed legs, I could've been dead.

And to be honest, that night, I didn't care if I was.

The girl whose house we were at had kicked me out after I threw up on her bed. Residual vomit sat on my unbuttoned khaki shirt while I was sprawled out in the hallway on my own, unconscious, as the party inside continued.

Earlier that day we had lost to the Giants reserves out at Blacktown. It was the most helpless I have ever felt on a football field. We scored 14 points to their 197. My former teammate Jed Lamb kicked eight goals.

One of the senior coaches, Alan, was at the game.

I could see him sitting towards the top of the grandstand. He had sunnies on top of his head and a black shirt on.

As we were taking our boots off after the match, he walked into the sheds. 'Listed boys, come with me,' he said, and so we walked into the adjacent room.

The door shut, and he stood next to a massage table while the rest of us formed a deflated semicircle around him. We were all looking down or away. Ashamed of what had just happened.

'At some point,' he said, with that tone of disappointment that lies beyond anger, 'you've got to start playing like men.'

I looked around at the rest of the group. Even though I was only in my third year, I was the most senior player there, so I spoke. 'It's just fucking shithouse,' I said. 'We can't wait until the ends of games for these conversations to happen. We should've hit each other with this out there. So, let's not wait till Monday for feedback, let's do it now.' And we went around the room and gave each other feedback on the game we had just played.

With the exception of a single quarter against Carlton, which I played after Heath Grundy pulled out minutes before the first bounce, it had been almost a year since my previous game of senior football. I had learned the hard truth that everything is inconsequential to performance in games. You can train the house down before pre-season starts, and top the GPS in pre-season, and not miss a session, and stand out in drills, but none of that matters if you don't take your chances when the bibs are put away and real opposition is introduced. They tell you that pre-season matters, but it only matters because games matter—a pre-season is a means to an end, and there's a difference between the guys who make their money as sparring partners, and the prize-fighters.

As the club had approached round one, we'd done a Leading Teams session in the Learning Centre. A large pad of butcher's paper sat up the front, and the white plastic chairs were arranged in rows. We split into groups and arranged the magnets of who we thought our best twenty-two were. The first thing my group had done was push the guys off to the side who we thought weren't in any kind of contention: the first-years and the injured players. Then the definites were put on the field. And then the crux of the exercise came: the placement of the middlemen. The cutting of the fringe. I sat waiting for my group to get to my name.

'Ahh, BJ.' A few of them looked at me. 'Yep, put him in.'

But that wasn't the norm across the groups. As group after group explained their choices, I saw my magnet off to the side in a two by two row with George Hewett and Daniel Robinson and Deano. The presenters all said something like, 'So we've got these guys off to the side because we think they're next in line. They could be in, and are doing everything right, but there's just no spots available.'

I sat there grinding my teeth.

Then, towards the end of the session, I raised my voice to one of the groups. 'Why aren't I in the team? I think I've done enough.'

There was a moment just before I spoke up where the words ran through my head and I thought it might be best not to say them. I think most players know what I'm talking about: when you're sitting in a meeting and say the answers in your head, but feel paralysed when you want to say them out loud. Then again, maybe that's just me.

But here I felt this upward pull, so I said it out loud. And now the room revolved around me. There were pins and needles in the back of my neck, and my cheeks felt how they do before I cry. Tensed. Made of steel.

Macca, sitting in his usual spot next to the pylon, spoke. 'Yeah look, you just haven't done enough with the opportunities you've had.'

Macca was probably the one person I would never bite back against. On the field he had a way of tilting his head and glaring that said more than words ever could, and in the changerooms he never let anyone get one over on him. He just didn't like losing at anything and was the epitome of being respected rather than liked. I could count the conversations he and I had had on one hand, but that doesn't matter—I still had him atop my leadership vote every year.

But I was at breaking point. So I snapped back at the captain of the club. 'Nah, in less minutes I've done more than those guys you've named.' As I spoke the words avalanched over themselves. 'More goals, touches, one-percenters. I've run further in pre-season. I've done more. I've done more.'

Each word came out faster than that which preceded it, and by the end of the run-on I needed to stop myself to catch my breath.

I looked at Macca. He didn't say anything, just shook his head as though he'd said everything he possibly could. If he came back at me I was going to go again.

Then Horse interjected. 'BJ, what have we spoken to you about?'

He was to my left. Behind Macca.

'I've got to improve my tank and finishing,' I mumbled, lacking the venom I had just spat out.

I didn't agree with either criticism at the time. I wanted to say that I had improved both aspects, and that I still wasn't getting enough opportunities. I wanted to say that the development group had identified me as the toughest trainer at the club and that after one NAB Cup game a Lions player said that I was a cunt to play on because I didn't stop moving the whole time. I had printed out the GPS numbers from the entire pre-season and kept them in my locker, ready to show Horse, though I never did. I wanted to bring all this up in the meeting right then, but suddenly I felt like I was wasting everyone's time, and that maybe I was the only person in the room who wasn't seeing the obvious: I wasn't good enough.

'Alright,' said Horse. 'Well, that's what we've said. You've got to keep working on it, alright?'

I had forgotten our rule of not taking feedback personally in those meetings, but it's a bit hard to remove yourself when all you want is to be in the team. I don't know if I wanted to play in the team, but I wanted to be in the team. I wanted proof that I was good enough.

When I walked out of the meeting Reggie walked beside me. 'Hey, that was good,' he said.

'You reckon?'

'Oh yeah, it's good to see someone care that much about it.'

A couple weeks later I sat in the crowd at ANZ Stadium watching Isaac Heeney play what ended up being a fairytale debut in round one. Every time he went near the ball I hoped it would bounce the other way, but the more I willed against him the better he seemed to play. That's the level of superstition I'd reached. I sat counting his stats in my head, telling myself that if he didn't get any more to half-time then they might drop him, thinking that if I didn't move then he wouldn't touch the ball. In the final minutes of the game, I knew he was going to kick an important goal, and I would've been the only person in red-and-white who'd wished he hadn't.

———

After Alan walked out of the changerooms at Blacktown, I grabbed my towel and headed to the showers.

The shower after a game washes away all the physical reminders of the past two hours: the dirt, the blood, the grass, the white paint. It would be nice if the thoughts of the game washed away with them. Washed away like flakes of dead skin. But most footballers aren't built like that. We replay the game in our heads; we ruminate; we scrutinise and search for the perfection that will never be. We say we leave it all out on the field, but the mental demons from games stay with us long after the final siren sounds. We are slaves to the past, always looking to do better the following week, staring at the ceiling after games, unable to sleep. Panadeine Forte normally helps. Or endone.

In the showers I rocked from side to side, letting the water bounce off my shoulders. Across from me were Mark and Blake, who I started talking to about the house party we'd been invited to that night. Blake knew the host, a woman named Jess, who was having people over to her apartment in Coogee, and he'd asked her if Mark and I could come. She said sure. We rarely went to house parties with people outside football. In 2015 it was always just to one of the boys' houses and then on to El Topo in Bondi Junction. Both Mark and Blake were rookie-listed, which meant they weren't in contention for seniors unless someone suffered a long-term injury.

As such, they were always ready to come out with me whenever I wanted to drink.

I made sure they were both still keen for that evening, then tied my boots to my bag and walked out of the room.

When I arrived home from the game, I had another shower. I sat down with my back against the tiles and watched water fall between my legs. There was still dirt on my knees and beneath my fingernails.

It was past the midpoint of the season, and I still hadn't played seniors. I'd started thinking about the reality that my career would be over at the end of the year when my contract was up. I felt like I had an expiration date. Each year I'd been at the club new players had come in with blank slates and proven themselves, while I was still yet to do that and felt like everything I did was being viewed as a reason not to pick me to play.

While all these thoughts were running through my head I heard my phone vibrate on the bathroom basin. I stood up and wiped away the fog on the shower screen to see who it was from, but I couldn't tell. When I got out I saw it was a text from my older brother Rhys, who I hadn't spoken to since Christmas.

———

After my third game in the AFL, Kieren and I stood in the middle of the MCG and did a TV interview together. We were both smiling, and I said something like, 'If I can be half the player he is, I'll be doing alright.'

During that following week Gerard Whateley made the comment that he wished there was a brother-brother rule in the AFL. 'To see brothers playing together in the same team,' he said, 'rather than as opposing forces—I love it.'

As the youngest of three boys I lived with a constant reverence for my older brothers. Everything they did was other-worldly to me, and I didn't know why but I always wanted to impress them.

My life was guided by the results of their infant wrestle with my parents. They had carved out a path that I would follow, as the lessons learned from and by them in the back-and-forth with our mum and dad were thrust onto me. I lived in their hand-me-down football jerseys, snuck into their rooms when they were out to look under their beds, and memorised the ink-pen etchings on the fronts of their school diaries which I then inscribed onto my own years later.

The truth is I've always felt guilty about playing Australian rules football.

Guilty because to me it felt like an act of abandonment. Not to my father, or my name—but I felt like I was making a choice between my older brothers. I felt like I was leaving Rhys on his own, stranded on a burning ship as he tried to get to the place that our father had been.

As a teenager, I'd watch him play lower grades for the Canterbury Bulldogs. I'd sit nervously hoping for him to do well, feeling as though his game was my own. My heart rate would elevate when the ball was in his hands and I'd wait for him to do his show-and-go move as he approached the line. Mum and Dad would be next to me, cheering him on, while also criticising his teammates who had previously taken his spot under their breath.

When I first arrived at the Swans, Kieren, Rhys and I lived together in Kieren's house on Canberra Street. In one of our first weeks as roommates Rhys and I went out for dinner in Coogee together and I talked about being at the footy club and how there were little things I could do to impress everyone.

'It's all about creating an image for yourself,' I said. 'Like, I know that a guy like Mike Pyke will value seeing me doing extra recovery and stretching, so I make sure I do it.'

We both ordered burgers and Rhys tried to talk about things outside football, because he was in a stage where his relationship with sport was unsettled, and in his expanding worldview he was reducing it—the thing we had geared our entire lives towards—to a mere phase of life. But my head had been fixed only on football since I'd walked into the Swans.

After a few months of all us living together, Rhys moved out.

It came shortly after the night when he went on a downward spiral because he couldn't find any nail clippers in the house. He paced around, searching everywhere.

'Don't worry,' I said. 'They'll be around here somewhere.' I don't think he heard me.

He eventually sat at the base of the stairs that went up to Kieren's bedroom, his face red and flustered.

I knew my brother had experienced struggles with his mental health, though of course we never spoke about it.

I first noticed it when it when I was lying beside him on a bed in Terrigal watching college football, after he'd had a shoulder reconstruction in 2009. His arm was in a sling and he was lying on his back propped up by pillows. There was a gloom around him, a sense of weight like I hadn't felt before.

There was a conversation which seemed to be growing closer and closer, but at the time I kept hoping that he would get to play at least one first-grade game before that conversation came. Just one, so that he could say he did it, because I thought that might make things alright for him.

After he stopped playing footy, Rhys and I would go down to Edward Bennett Park and play a game with an AFL ball and a rugby league ball. We'd set up two squares about forty metres apart, and we'd each stand in one. We'd then take turns kicking from one square to the other. If you landed it in the other person's square, probably a three-metre-by-three-metre target, you'd get a point. Rhys' kicking technique was never fluid. His left forearm would twist and end up facing towards the target, meaning his hand would be at the back of the ball, usually towards the top. As the ball would fall down to his foot, it would tilt slightly, meaning the sweet spot wasn't as big—he was still a handy kick though. Whenever we played this game at the park I would deliberately pull my kicks so that I didn't win, and I always felt he did the same, because drawing out the game meant that we could spend more time together.

———

In 2014, Rhys wrote a piece about alcohol-fuelled violence. I was so impressed by the nuance of his take and the delicate way he had constructed his argument. In the first article I ever wrote I included a line from it, and we had a fight because he didn't want me to use it without crediting him, but the commissioning editor said that they'd rather not do that. I took the quote, and his name, out.

I often thought about quitting professional football in my first year because of the impact I felt it was having on Rhys. He never said anything to me, but I had noticed that every time I'd progressed—made my debut, kicked my first goal—I'd get a call from Dad the following week and somewhere in the conversation he'd say something like, 'Rhys isn't doing well.'

Sometimes I try to imagine how it would feel if Kieren and Rhys played football together and I had to watch on from the sidelines. If I had to sit at home and see them smiling at the camera, then running off with their hands on each other's backs as the commentators said how special it was to see them play together. I'm sure I'd tell people I was proud, and that I was happy for them, and all those other magnanimous things you're meant to say when someone else is living out your dream, but I know I would've felt uneasy deep down. I'm sure part of me would want to scream out, 'I'm here too, don't forget about me!' Not to a crowd, or to the public, but to my brothers.

But I don't know if he's ever felt that. I'm projecting. That says more of me than him.

What I do know is that we have not been in contact since the message he sent me that day in 2015 and that our beliefs are not aligned on certain values. Originally it seemed to be a conflict between his religious awakening and newfound biblical morality—which I became aware of via a letter I received prior to Christmas in 2014, when he asked me to come home for the holiday after hearing I would not be there—and its incongruence with my own search for freedom. But the situation has moved beyond that incongruence; beyond any one incident, and has become an incompatibility where silence seems to suit us both best.

Each of us are entitled to hold our own views; one of us is no more correct than the other, and to fight to make it so would do little to help, but what I find myself most fixated on is how the moments he has chosen to strike—me with that text after my worst loss; Kieren with an open letter published on the day of his final game—have arrived at the peaks and troughs of our footballing lives, as though the game exposes emotional vulnerabilities which allow the knife to be driven deeper. To me, it speaks of a deeply ingrained, perhaps unconscious, valuing of football. Something which may have come from years of walking past the wall of photographs by the stairs of our childhood home.

Instead of lynching the perpetrator, we should look at the culture which created him.

That was the line he wrote that I took out of the article. It concerns itself with sociology, which I now have a degree in.

The last time Rhys and I saw each other was at our grandfather's funeral. He sat up the front, beside Mum and Dad, and I sat up the back. Often when I walk down the street I'll see someone who I think looks like my brother. I always stare at the person and wait for them to look back at me. I study their legs because he always had bandy legs, like Dad. As the person comes closer my heart begins to race and I imagine what they'd say if they were him. But I don't remember how his voice sounds. It's been too long. I know that he is married, and that he runs a blog where he posts motivational articles about letting go and holding no regrets and that he says he is grateful for the lessons he learned from his football career.

Now that I think about it, it makes sense that Rhys found God when he did, if only for a brief period of time. When people turn to religion later in life, I feel it is not without prompt. Used to fill a hole, or soothe despair, or give meaning where it is not currently felt. He found his coping mechanism, and I would soon find mine.

Growing up, people said I looked like a mix of my brothers, though the older I get, the more I think I look like Rhys in the face. Sometimes when I look at myself in the mirror, I see parts of him looking back.

———

After reading Rhys' text I threw my phone on the bed and walked towards the kitchen of the apartment. I was too tired to cry. But I wanted to be numb, so I took an empty fruit-juice bottle from the recycling bin and filled it with whatever alcohol I could find. You see, alcohol lowers your blood sugar, and if you pass out as a diabetic and people think it's because you're drunk and wait for you to come around in the morning, then you might never wake up. I knew that, and while it wasn't the endpoint I sought, it was not one that I tried to avoid in the endeavour to drive myself into oblivion so that the pain I was feeling went away.

Then I took a six-pack of ciders from the fridge, stuck a knife in the bottom of a can and shotgunned it. I did the same thing, can after can. After the fourth I put my head in the sink and stared into the drain below. The noise of my own dry retching hit the metal around me and reverberated into my ears. I turned the tap on and pushed the chunks of vomit down the sink with my fingers.

By the time we got to the party I was already on another planet. When we walked through the front door I remember seeing a guy on the couch googling the rules of King's Cup while the rest of the people in the room sat cross-legged on the floor without drinks in their hands. I sat on the couch and proceeded to drink from the bottle of alcohol I had brought. I could hear laughter and voices and spotted Mark and Blake standing on the other side of the room.

Later on, there was a woman in the kitchen who I approached while gripping a bottle of fireball whiskey in my hand. Her name was Ashleigh, and I recognised her from a video that had gone viral a few years earlier where she made her eyebrows dance to some electronic song.

'So, what do you do?' she asked.

'I'm a pool cleaner,' I said.

She laughed, so I think she knew I was joking. She then said something about being a basketballer, and I don't think she'd ever played basketball before.

I raised the bottle of fireball in my hand and asked if she wanted to do a shot.

'Sure,' she said.

I poured out two shots of fireball. We cheersed and drank.

Without asking, I poured a second round and handed it to her.

'Oh no, I'm okay,' she said, so I drank both.

I did that again. And then a fourth time.

I kept drinking until I couldn't walk, and I was kicked out after I threw up on Jess' bed. When the party was over, Blake and Mark found me in the corridor, took me home and carried me into my room.

The next morning, the boys came and picked me up and we went to Big W in Eastgardens so I could buy new bedsheets for Jess. At the shops we saw Ashleigh.

'Hell-o,' she said, holding the 'o' at the end. 'How's your head today?'

Sheepishly I said that I was all good.

I bought the sheets, plus some red ribbon to tie around them, and wrote 'Sorry' on a little piece of paper that I attached.

Jess was hesitant about letting me in to her house until I held the new bedsheets up to the peephole in the door.

When I gave them to her she said thanks. We haven't spoken since. I think she's signed a record deal with Sony or something now. I know she opened for Coldplay a few years back.

I lay in bed that night feeling hopeless in a way that I hadn't experienced before. This was my first experience of the depression that comes after drinking. The night before I'd taken today's happiness and used it up, only I couldn't even remember the happiness that I had stolen.

The next morning I fumbled my way through a touch session and then almost threw up after our recovery run. My CK reading—a creatine kinase test which measures the breakdown of your muscles from the weekend—was so high that it was unable to be read. The machine said, *Dilute*.

The reserves coaches didn't give a summary of our game to the rest of the group in the meeting that afternoon. Horse said it was just a really disappointing effort and that for the seniors to win a flag we needed the reserves to be firing. Then he singled me out in front of the team. 'BJ—where's BJ?'

I raised my hand.

'Okay, there you are,' he said, looking me in the eyes. It felt like we were the only people in the room. 'You know, you're the only one who can hold your head high from that game. You had a crack.'

I'd had twenty-five touches and ten tackles.

So, life went on.

Ashleigh and I hung out a couple of times. She asked me to put glow-in-the-dark stickers on the ceiling of her bedroom and I got her tickets to a game I played a few weeks later. She had something else on that night, I think.

SPRAY-PAINTED GREEN

My weeks started to revolve around the words in Wednesday afternoon text messages.

The texts were usually sent around 5pm and would tell me I was in either an 8.30am or 9.15am team meeting the following morning. The 8.30am text meant that I was in the senior squad of 25, though there were usually closer to 30 in that room, as injured players and guys passing 'go' in the reserves for match fitness sat in too.

In the 8.30am meeting I'd sit in my usual spot, four seats in from the steel drinking fountain which was pressed into the right-hand corner of the room—next to where Mike Pyke used to sit—and directly in front of Joey, with a spiral-bound orange notebook open in my lap. In it I would write down everything that was said. Things like, 'Richmond likes to possess the footy. Really high uncontested marking team, so we will have to shorten our teasing distance. Cotchin and co. not dangerous in the back half.' And 'Western Bulldogs play without fear—they just flick it around with hands and hit whoever is open. Are big on outnumbering at the scramble, so don't get caught in between. If you can get over and help, go in.' And 'Hawthorn will drop off our 5th player running in to the centre bounce. Make sure the 6th rounds them up. Sit off their left leg for left-footers.'

The meeting was usually orchestrated by Stuey Maxfield, who would scout the opposition teams during the week. We'd talk about their kick-in and zone set-ups, how they got a spare back, what they were likely to do if we had a spare back; ultimately we'd reduce their existence as a football team down to a few words, and we would will ourselves to see a fragility in those words. Then we would talk about what we would do to counteract what they presented. As a team we were very reactionary. The classic example of this was 'wing on wing'. At centre bounces, our wingers usually had no other plan than to run in next to their opponents, or hold out if that's what their opponents did. Our game plan rarely changed because we had a system that we trusted to work in most cases: team defence. If we got our team defence right then teams would be strangled, and we'd hurt them on turnover. With the ball we didn't really have much strategy—just switch and hit the runners, then get it in to Bud. Defence was the priority. Always.

We'd have a similar meeting in the afternoon, where we'd go through clips from training that showed where we'd done what we wanted to do on the weekend. In the clips you could often hear Horse, or the other coaches, clapping and cheering at the end. Much of the point of these afternoon meetings was to leave on Thursdays feeling like we could win.

The 9.15 message meant I was in the reserves meeting. When I was in this meeting I'd try to arrive just after the senior squad had climbed the stairs to go into the Learning Centre. I didn't like the feeling of being left alone in the changeroom as players converged before they decided to head upstairs together, and I didn't like passing them on their way up.

In the reserves meeting we'd do a simplified version of the senior meeting, focusing only on what the opposition team would do, rather than ways to counteract it, so that we could replicate the way they played in our match simulation drill we called 18 vs 18. Overall the reserves meetings were more relaxed, sometimes starting with a joke or game of hangman using an old player's name, like 'Ronnie Burns'. We'd already be in our training kit and have our ankles taped, and we didn't sit in our usual seats. The room was near-empty some weeks and it didn't feel like there was a whole lot of pressure on us.

At the start of the 9.15am meeting, the development coaches would look out and say, 'Alright, we need a . . .' and they'd peer out at the assortment of players before them and assign roles as target players. Over the years I was assigned to play as Eddie Betts, Stephen Hill, Bradley Hill, Cyril Rioli, Daniel Wells, Chad Wingard and Luke Breust. Originally, I thought it was a tick against your name to be a target player; it gave you the freedom to do whatever you wanted in the drill most of the time. But then again, it meant you were in the reserves wearing a yellow bib, when the goal always was to not wear a bib.

————

Two weeks after the night where I tried to drink myself into oblivion in Coogee, I received the Wednesday afternoon text saying 8.30am. We were set to play Hawthorn at ANZ

Stadium, the ground that had hosted the Sydney Olympics, where they now used green spray-paint to cover patches of dirt and sand so that it looked like grass on TV.

After being told I was in the senior team, I wore a pair of newspaper-mâché-grey-and-neon-green-tick Nike Tiempos to Thursday's training. I knew I'd wear them in the weekend's game because Horse hated it when blokes fell over—like, really hated it—and on the unstable, crumbly ANZ Stadium surface I didn't trust my moulds. The surface was inconsistent, not only on the flanks where the grandstands had been pulled back after games of rugby league, but in the middle too.

The grey Tiempos were the only pair of boots with steel screw-in studs that I owned. I had four pairs of boots that year—that's all my Nike deal entitled me to (plus two pairs of runners). For guys like me, there was no money in such deals, or merch (hoodies, tees, shorts, tracksuits)—just a few pairs of boots that you ordered in twice a year. Some of the top guys would change boots every few weeks, and also be paid a few thousand dollars to play in a certain brands. The running joke at the club was that every year XBlades would throw the kitchen sink at a few blokes—if any of the bigger name players wore something that wasn't Asics, Adidas, Puma or Nike then we all assumed there'd been a fair sum involved.

After the 8.30am meeting the coaches came up and patted me on the back for my performances in the twos. They said that getting the call-up again was a credit to all the hard work I'd done in the pre-season. I felt wanted again. Which was nice.

When I arrived at ANZ Stadium with Kieren before the game, I finally felt like I was ready to be an AFL footballer. I was fitter and stronger than I'd ever been, and I'd put up consistently good numbers in the reserves. I felt like I'd never properly earned my spot before, but this time I was hardened, and had fought for what was now mine.

When I took the field, Ben Stratton started whacking me in the back, screaming out, 'YEAH!' every time he did. I remember that I kept moving in small figure eights so that he couldn't hit me easily. I remember that when he screamed out he looked like a madman—like a fucking lunatic. But it wasn't intimidating, just confusing. We were beaten badly. Hawthorn's foot skills cut us up all over the ground. I think Bud kicked a couple of quick goals at one stage, but outside that it was a bleak night on the field.

Kieren dropped me home after the game, and when I got out of the car he leaned across Charlotte, who was sitting in the passenger's seat, and with his head angled up towards me through the window, said, 'Hey mate, good game tonight, I'm proud of you.'

I could hear in his voice that he was tired and sore.

I think I had eighteen disposals.

I thought I'd done enough to keep my spot.

———

In review meetings, you could tell when a clip you were in was coming up, and you knew why it was being shown.

I never believed players who when watching a clip of themselves said they didn't know where they were on the field, or what was going through their head.

Sometimes Horse would say something like, 'Is that you Jonesy?' or 'What are you doing here, Deano?' and Jonesy or

Deano, or whoever, would reply, 'Ahh, I can't tell,' or 'I'm not sure,' and it always felt like a lie. There was this collective recall that we all had—I say we because straight after games we'd exchange stories from the field and the same would happen on Monday—so you knew that guys knew.

The Monday after the Hawks game, a clip was played where Shaun Burgoyne took a mark in the middle of the ground with no one on him. The heading on the previous slide had read, 'Team Defence.' I knew from the moment the still frame appeared that this was a clip about me. And sure enough, at the bottom of the screen I had just crept into frame as Burgoyne took the mark. The green dot from the laser pointer in Horse's hand had followed Burgoyne's lead and circled around where he now held the ball. In that moment all I could think was, *Everyone can fucking see it. Everyone thinks I'm fucking soft. Fucking lazy. They don't respect me.*

I had the choice to either speak up, which would soften the blow a bit, or to not say anything and hope a big deal wasn't made about it.

I cleared my throat, like I always did before speaking in those review meetings. 'Yeah, that was shithouse by me.' *Shithouse by me* was stock rhetoric in those meetings.

Horse turned and looked at me.

I continued, 'I can't give him that much distance. I was too slow to get over, and then I didn't make him earn it, either. I've got to at least take him to ground.'

The next clip played.

I slumped into my chair, hoping that I wouldn't appear in any more clips, knowing the moments where I might, and hoping that none of the still frames matched up to those moments.

The next day I did my individual game review with Vince. Every player did one of these with their line coach each week. Vince would pull fifteen or so clips from the game, and there'd be words down the bottom that described what was going on. Things like, *BJ. Defence. Off ball. Missed tackle.* or *BJ. Reaction time.*

He showed me the clips, skipping over the one that had come up in the meeting the day before, making sure I knew that it was the one I'd already seen, as though I didn't remember exactly what happened after that single still frame of players arranged on the field.

At the end of the final clip the screen went black and returned to the start screen which had the frames of play layered over each other as squares. Vince turned to me, leaned back in his chair and took his time with his words. 'Obviously it's up in the air this week. I can't really tell you too much outside of that.'

Vince always seemed like he was giving you space to reply, but in my position the answers were usually clear.

He continued, 'You've just got to make sure that when you get a chance, you take it.'

'Okay,' I said, and stayed seated for a few seconds before walking out.

———

All that week I felt like shit. I'd been given another chance and I'd wasted it. I could do extra things during the week, and train well, but none of it mattered. The only salvation I could hope for would be found in the upcoming weekend's senior game, but that wasn't possible because I wasn't playing. I'd been dropped.

Still, I was taken to Perth as an emergency for the seniors and on the day of the game against West Coast, Bud pulled out with a tight back. Horse came up and told me I was going to come in to the team. 'You'll play a full game, and Tommy will stay as sub because we want your pace in the forward line on the bigger deck.'

After that, Vince came up to me in the team room at the hotel and said, 'Let's just run over a few more edits before the game so you're set.' We walked over to his laptop which was set up on a table and watched clips from the game the week before that framed my performance more positively.

———

At three-quarter-time Horse pulled us all into a huddle. We were playing poorly. He looked around, trying to find eye contact.

'We're being led by two young blokes right now, BJ and Heenz. It's time for more guys to jump on.'

Before we broke, the guys all geed each other up, grabbing the jerseys of the guys beside them and shaking them in their fists. When we walked out into our positions, I grabbed Heenz and said, 'You and me have to keep going, alright?' and he nodded his head at me.

I kicked two goals and had fifteen disposals and five or six tackles, but we lost by fifty points. After the game we walked solemnly into the coaches' room, sapped, deflated. Two big losses in a row, something we weren't accustomed to.

Horse stood up the front and singled me out. 'BJ, how often do you come into the club and do extra goalkicking?'

'Every day,' I said.

He looked around at the rest of the group, then back at me. 'And did it pay off today?'

'Yeah, it did.'

I was tired. There was dirt and emu oil on my legs. My eyes were stinging. But at least, I thought, I'd be getting a game next week.

Horse said one more thing right then.

'BJ, you'll get to the end of your career and will be able to say, "Well, I was this, and I was this, and yeah I wasn't really that—but I had a crack, and I left no stone unturned."'

When he finished he walked out of the room. Then, after a moment of silence, the rest of the coaches followed. The players sat for a bit longer—I was waiting for the lead of the senior guys—before moving.

The showers were a quiet affair—a lot of deep breaths, head-shaking and sighs. The ice baths at that ground were in green wheelie bins.

I sat next to Harry Cunningham on the bus to the swimming pool in Perth where we always did post-game recovery. 'I knew Horse was going to single you out,' he said.

Dinner was served in the team room at the hotel: burgers, steaks, chicken, the usual stuff. No one had the energy to play table tennis. I took two bottles of Gatorade from the fridge, rode the elevator to my room and went to sleep.

———

In the lead-up to the game the following week, Horse mentioned that Goodesy was taking leave from the playing group. It was a brief announcement, and Horse looked deeply saddened by it, but we quickly moved on to football.

For more than a year Goodesy had been booed by crowds for his stance against racism, and in the previous two weeks against Hawthorn and West Coast it'd escalated, wearing him down to the point where he didn't want to take the field at all anymore. Whenever Adam was near the ball, it was so loud; louder than I'd ever heard a crowd boo. And it was clearly pointed towards a single person.

Back in 2013, I was in a hotel room in Canberra with my reserves teammates watching our senior side play Collingwood. Goodesy was the best player on the field that game. We were all in awe of the way he moved and how he did things that no other player in our team could do. Since playing the majority of the Grand Final the year before on a busted PCL he hadn't dominated games the way he once did. But on this night in 2013, everything clicked. In full force, the dual Brownlow medallist tore the game open.

Adam defied belief on the field. He could put his knee in your back and win the ball in the air. He could bend down with one hand and pick the footy up off the deck without breaking stride. He was lightning fast. He was incredibly strong. He was fit. He was tough. He could kick equally as well with his left and right foot, and he had that unteachable X-factor that meant that as long as he was on the field, you could never count his team out. And to go with all this, he was an incredibly hard worker. A relentless professional. An unflinching yet compassionate leader, and a driver of standards with everything that he did.

All of this was on display that night and the newspaper match report would have been written and ready to go by the third-quarter break, full of talk about the return of Goodesy and speculation on how many more years he could play. Then, late in the fourth quarter, the ball went over the boundary line inside our forward 50. Goodesy followed the ball out, turned and went to run back to his position. But before crossing the line for the field of play, he stopped, turned back around and pointed to a person in the crowd. He motioned to a security guard to escort them out. The guard did not move. Goodesy took his mouthguard out and pointed again. I'd never seen anything like this before, none of us had. With one minute and fifty seconds left on the game clock, a Collingwood fan was escorted out by security up the aisle of the MCG. Adam then ran to the bench and sat down. You could tell he was trying to fully process what had just happened. Before the siren went he walked down to the rooms on his own. The person in the crowd was a girl, thirteen years of age, who had called him an ape.

The following day Goodesy stood in front of a media pack. He told them all—and everyone around the country—that he was gutted. That he was shattered by what had happened. He sought not to blame the young girl, saying that she was simply the by-product of a racist culture, and that this would be an opportunity for her to learn and grow.

'Racism had a face last night,' he said, 'and it was a thirteen-year-old girl, but it's not her fault. She's thirteen, she's still so innocent. I don't put any blame on her. Unfortunately, it's what she hears, the environment that she's grown up in that has made her think that it's okay to call people racist names.

I felt like I was in high school again, being bullied, being called all of these names because of my appearance. I didn't stand up for myself in high school, but I am a lot more confident now, I am a lot more proud about who I am and of my culture, and I decided to stand up last night and I will continue to stand up.'

He continued, 'The person that needs the most support right now is the little girl. People need to get around her. She's thirteen, she's uneducated. If she wants to pick up the phone and apologise, I'll take that phone call and I'll have a conversation with that girl about, you know what, you called me a name, this is how it made me feel.'

Goodesy looked tired. There were nine microphones right up in his face.

It was from this point on that the constant booing started.

———

I had never been drunk before my first boat cruise at the Swans. I was nervous, and things were exacerbated by the fact that Kieren, my safety blanket at the club, was bedridden with glandular fever. When I arrived at the backyard of one of my teammate's houses following our final training session of the year, I was handed a UDL to scull, which I did. We then got in a taxi and headed towards a wharf in Circular Quay where we boarded a boat that would sail around Sydney Harbour for the next four hours. On the boat, each of the first-year players had to sing a song on the karaoke machine—mine was a duet with Jake Lloyd of 'Holy Grail' by Hunters & Collectors. After the song finished, it was my turn to do the compulsory first-year scull. I was handed two glasses of vodka, and looked at them timidly. Goodesy walked over and stood next to me and asked if I was okay. He said I didn't have to drink if I didn't want too. He then he put his arm around my shoulders while the rest of my teammates cried out *scull, scull*.

There were many big names and premiership heroes at the Swans when I first arrived, but Adam was by far the biggest star. He was a two-time premiership player, a two-time Brownlow medallist, a five-time All-Australian, a three-time Bob Skilton Medallist (for the Swans Best and Fairest) and a member of the Indigenous Team of the Century. He had one of those lockers that you stood in front of and took your time reading: the sheer amount of white text imprinted onto his door was almost unbelievable.

Adam was a superstar, but the Adam I came to know sat upright and attentive at the front of every team meeting, with an aluminium drink bottle under his chair, forever hydrating, forever looking to do the little things right.

In one of my first weeks at the club, a group of us did a touch session (a series of handballing exercises at a frenetic pace) and Adam said, 'BJ, you and me, come on.'

I had been practising my touch in the dungeon, but still struggled with the pace we set, failing to seamlessly transition between lefts and rights and unders and overs. Most first-year players are like this—touch is a very particular type of football skill which relies on months of practice and muscle memory to perfect. When you finally grasp it, you are able to function as a cog in the machine, and there's a comfort in that. That day, Adam stood opposite me and was patient, even stopping mid-drill to give me some basic advice on my handballing technique. When I was handballing with my right hand I stood flat footed, not putting my left foot forward. It's a small detail, one he didn't need to point out, but it showed that he cared about me becoming a better player.

Superstars often have this unapproachable aura about them—usually unintentional. I think Adam knew this, and he went out of his way to make sure young players— and fans—weren't intimidated by him. Starstruck kids wanting his autograph would be too shy to ask, so he would bend down, put his eyes at their level, and make them feel they could speak to him. Then he'd always make sure they said thank you, but he wouldn't pry it out of them.

He had a soothing demeanour; his eyes met yours as if he understood you and he focused on you when you spoke, and his voice provided a calming respite in an often ferocious footy environment. The way he smiled, showing you his teeth and gums, made you want to smile too.

Even when you fucked up, he knew how to manage it without the heavy-handedness of other leaders. The week before I made my debut, I didn't tell the physios that I had hurt my knee. Adam overheard the physios talking about it and he brought it up with the leadership group that afternoon, but he didn't mention my name. He said that a young player had done something unprofessional, so it was the right time for the leaders to reinforce our standards. Kieren connected the dots and told me that Goodesy had protected me. He had a sense of compassion, and timing. If he used my name then I wouldn't've played the following week, as undermining the club's culture would've been an easy reason for the coaches not to pick me.

One day Adam and I were walking to our cars after training, and we stood in front of the P.J. Gallagher's Irish Pub at

Moore Park. There had been a riddle circulating the change-rooms that day and Adam posed it to me: 'BJ, I'm having a party. Certain things can come, and certain things cannot. Beer can come, but wine can't. Glass can, but the window can't. Wood can, timber can't.'

I had no idea what the answer was, so I started guessing. 'Plants can come, but grass can't?'

Wrong.

'Water can come, but the ocean can't?'

Wrong again.

Goodesy smirked and pointed to the words 'Gallagher's' and 'Guinness' on the signage of the pub. They could both come, he said, but apparently Guinness could *really* come. He gave me just enough so that I could figure it out for myself.

'The door can come but the handle can't,' I said.

Goodesy laughed. 'That's it, bruz: double letters.'

The week that Adam took leave from the playing group, I arrived at the SCG for the Adelaide Crows game. Walking through the sea of people on Driver Avenue, I saw a sign that said there would be a minute of applause in the seventh minute of the third quarter in support of Goodesy—his guernsey number being 37.

I was on the bench when the minute of applause began. The hairs on the back of my neck stood up. Then when it finished the crowd sat back down, and the game went on.

FUCK

I was in Perth in my hotel room packing my bag to get on the bus for the game and I couldn't find my mouthguard.

I tipped my travel bag upside down and scattered its contents on the floor. A towel. A spare pair of boots. Training shorts. Two singlets. A couple of books. A grey t-shirt. My New Balance casual shoes with the rubber soles hanging loose.

Where the fuck is it, I thought. *It has to be here, fuck.*

I checked under the bed, I checked in the front pocket of my backpack, I checked in my boots. My toiletries bag. The bathroom basin. I even checked in the small wire-framed bin beneath the desk.

I checked everywhere. And it wasn't there, and I was overcome with anxiety as the voice in my head started yelling, *Fuck, fuck, fuck.*

It was the morning of my ninth game in a row for the senior team, and my first-ever finals game. And I had forgotten my fucking mouthguard.

I looked up where the closest chemist was on my phone and went to get an Uber from out the front of the hotel. While I was waiting, Joey asked where I was going.

'I didn't bring my fucking mouthguard,' I said, looking lost and distressed. 'I need to go get one.'

Joey replied, 'Mate, I've got a spare you can use if you want?'

Relief. 'Fuck, that would be great,' I said.

Joey took me up to his room and rifled through his bag. I was standing between the mini-fridge and the bathroom. He pulled out a Shock Doctor mouthguard and ripped it out of its plastic casing. He read out the instructions. There was a powder and a gel that we had to mix together with a flat plastic stick. Once mixed into a semi-rubbery substance, we lined it on the inside of the mouthguard. I then placed the mouthguard in my mouth, bit down and clenched my teeth for about a minute. Then I took it out of my mouth and put it in a glass of cold water.

Joey asked how I was feeling, and I said I was ready. Which was a lie.

I put the mouthguard in my mouth again. It sort of fit, but it didn't cling to my teeth like a dentist's mould did. There were scraps of the dried rubber coming off the edges. I moved my jaw from side to side and flared my teeth and felt it slipping around, and when I tried to talk with it in my words were muffled.

I thanked Joey and said it would do.

While we sat on the bus out the front of the hotel, there was a fight between two strangers in the street. One was a cab driver, I think. We pressed our noses against the window. I felt like chaos was following me. On the way to the game all I could think about was how I couldn't yell with this mouthguard in. Not being able to yell and use your voice on the field made you a passenger.

We lost that game, and in my review meeting that week Vince showed me a clip where I fumbled in the goal square. He pressed pause. 'Did you have a look at the defender there?' he asked.

I didn't respond.

'It's finals footy, can't be soft like that.' Then he did the lean-back, hands on his head, intimating once again that *It's up in the air* . . .

That was the last game in which I ever wore a mouthguard.

———

I got a phone call from Horse while at Bondi Junction the afternoon before the following game, which was a do-or-die semifinal.

'BJ, we're going with Rosey this week,' he said. 'We think he gives us more firepower up forward.'

Rosey had only played one quarter of senior football up to that point, but had kicked three goals in that quarter. I didn't say much back. When the conversation finished I bought a leather-bound blank journal from the newsstand in front of me.

When I got home I sat on the lounge in the living room and called Kieren. I cried when I told him I was out. He said that it was just a part of the journey. Then I called Rosey and said I was proud of him and that I didn't want things to become weird between us because he had taken my spot. He said thanks, and that the phone call really meant a lot because he did feel bad that I was dropped for him.

'Nah, mate, that's just footy,' I said.

After talking to Rosey I wrote 'New beginnings' in the front of the journal I had just bought.

———

At the hotel before the game I made a ham, cheese, lettuce and tomato sandwich which I Glad Wrapped and then placed in a brown paper bag. Shawry sat down next to me.

'How are you feeling, bud, ready to play?'

'Nah, I'm not playing,' I said.

His eyes shot out of his head in surprise.

We all drove from the hotel to the car park beneath the ground. I was the last to get taped and didn't bother putting my name down for a massage. I just watched. I watched Rampe cross-legged with his headphones in, and Smooch in his seat still wearing his polo and slacks while everyone else got changed. I watched the coaches go around to the players and give them their final notes. I watched them all pass by the table with paper cups of Gatorade and water on top.

When the team went out for the warm-up I took a Sherrin and did a few groundballs against the wall and a couple of kicks into the large nets that draped down from the roof of the adjacent room. After fifteen minutes I heard the boys coming back down the race. 'Foot on their fucking throats!' was being yelled out amid the sound of leather bouncing on concrete and catchcries of 'Four quarters of ruthless Bloods footy!'

We all went into the room for one last address from Horse. The others all ate their gels and drank from their bottles and I sat in the back corner. They walked out onto the ground and I sat in the changerooms and ripped my ankle tape off. When the ball was bounced one of the trainers came in and gave me the all-clear, but I was already in my slacks by then.

I left immediately after the final siren went. A group of us who weren't playing went straight to a car and cracked a few UDLs one of them had stashed in the boot before the game. With a drink in my hand, I read online that Goodesy had retired and I announced it to the rest of the car.

We had Silly Sunday at a place in Loch Maree Street, and the police came because we had a bonfire in the backyard. Then Mad Monday ended up at ScuBar, where I snuck in a large live Alaskan king crab to put in the middle of the hermit crab races. For a dollar, you could name one of the crabs, and the announcer would call that name out during the race. The crowd chanted out, 'USAIN CRAB' in between renditions of the Carlton Blues club song—we'd heard rumours that Tom Mitchell was going to sign with them. Sam Reid had a black top on and roped off an area, pretending to be a security guard. Long cheers of 'GOOOOOODESY' and 'SHAAAAWRY' rang out across the bar for the two major senior players retiring.

I stood at a table with Shawry and he told me he was going to coach at the Swans the following year. 'You're the bloke I'm most excited about coaching,' he said to me. 'No offence to you guys,' he added to Marshy and Deano, who were standing beside us, 'but BJ is my favourite.' He went on to tell me he thought it was weird that Horse had made that comment about the end of my career after the West Coast game. 'You're only twenty-one!' he said. We both laughed.

On Wednesday night we all went to El Topo and there was a booth behind the DJ reserved for Bernard Tomic—at least that's what the A4 piece of paper taped to the table said. We railroaded the booth. Bernard never turned up.

I was drunk, and dancing, and approaching the euphoric phase of an alcohol-drenched night. Then I started crying in the middle of the dance floor. Sobbing. Bawling my eyes out. I'd looked over at Lloyd Perris who had been delisted that day after doing his knee twice in the previous two years. The year before he'd cried in our joint end-of-year review. He could've played AFL football, but just never got the chance.

Kieren grabbed me and we walked down the stairs. We got in the back of a cab together and I started screaming, 'It's not fair, it's not fucking fair!'

In the moment I was talking about Lloyd, but I know now there was more to it than that. The illusion of being a professional footy player had worn off for me.

But I had just signed a two-year contract.

———

About six months ago Lloyd and I sat on my balcony in Randwick reading through my old journals. I showed him something I'd written about him right after he played his first game since doing his knee in the last session before Christmas in 2014. After the first line, he shot his arm towards me and put his hand on my knee and started crying. I ripped out the pages and gave them to him.

'Keep them,' I said. 'They're yours.'

Then we stared out over the bus depot and had a drink and joked about the 2014 NEAFL final and how in 2011 we lined up against each other on the wing at Olds Park.

PART III

DOM

Dom has a black cable coiled around his neck and a microphone gripped in his right hand which he punches into the air on the accents of the crash cymbal. His ear is pierced by a gold hoop and his head is shaved. He reminds me of people I've never met, people like Ian Curtis, or the singer from Black Flag, Henry Rollins.

Before the show I talked to Dom in the venue hallway. He spoke softly and said that he had been crying that afternoon. Now I watch as his eyes roll up into the back of his head and his mouth swings between the words he spits out. With jilted legs and an arched back he looks possessed; Dom doesn't just sing, he shouts, he lets something out, something unfiltered, untainted, pure. There are nine people in the crowd, standing in a semicircle around the band. The drum kit is on a small stage and the amps are pushed to the corners of the room. A guy from a party on the balcony walks past and looks through the door. I see him raise his eyebrows as Dom screams. He doesn't get it. This band is cathartic. A performance piece of fearlessness and unabashed primordialism.

Grace stands beside me and I reach for her hand. When we arrived tonight I told her that this was where I came after I met her for the first time three years ago. Her band had played at the Chippendale Hotel, which is just down the road, and I was standing in the crowd next to Dicko—Ian Dickson, the white-haired British judge from Australian Idol—as my drummer was trying to tackle me to the ground.

'Fuck off,' I kept saying, getting ready to hit the drunken mess in the face with my closed fist. We had just recorded our EP and he'd been drinking since 10am.

'Hey, we love him,' Dicko said to me, seeing how pissed-off I was, trying to calm the situation down. 'You've got to let him be, he's an asset. People will love him.'

I let him be. That was our final night as a band.

Music had been at the periphery of my childhood—Kieren had played guitar and I would sneak into his room and flip through the plastic sheets filled with six lined tabs printed on A4 paper from bands like the Red Hot Chili Peppers and Metallica; but he and I would never sit around and talk about bands or listen to anything outside what was on the radio. I was drawn to music. When I was ten years old my mother took me to buy my first guitar—a three-quarter size nylon string Valencia which cost ninety dollars—and I spent the dwindling hours of that day locked inside my room learning single note melodies and chords until the tips of my fingers started to wear.

So strong was my affinity with the guitar that after that first day I woke up in the middle of the night screaming because my neck had jarred from being constantly crooked as I stared down at the fretboard. I would play and play and play, but in the years that followed, I would rarely—if ever—play in front of people, only to myself, and I would always sing quietly under my breath or in the shower, drowned out by the water. It wasn't until I saw a Kurt Cobain documentary in 2015 that my obsession with music became more than a private fixation. The song that hooked me was 'Territorial Pissings'. Kurt's vocals come in after a machine gun drum fill. The guitar sounds like metal is being scraped across its strings. Then in the outro, Kurt just screams. That was it for me. Those screams.

To fill the void that came from my disillusionment with football I started writing songs every day, and I sent away demos to labels and radios stations, hoping for a reply. I had no idea what I was doing, and I liked that. I didn't know how to double guitars, or that the kick and bass should be lined up, or that harmonies could exist low in the mix. I liked the unfamiliarity and visceral estrangement of it all. I liked my naivety. Music for me was—and still is—an introverted experience. An independence. A liberation. I'd come home from footy training and lock myself in my room and make music until I went to sleep. It was something that I could have and my teammates couldn't. It was my way of saying 'I don't belong here.'

Dicko got involved after he heard one of my demos. He said he was a big fan of the punk stuff I was making. 'It's proper punk,' he'd say, 'it makes my blood boil.'

He asked me to send him new songs as I wrote them and I'd usually send at least two a week. He told me I was prolific and he liked my lyricism, except one time he called me after he'd had a drink and said something like, 'Not your best' about a song I'd sent him that was a White Stripes rip off. The next day he called and apologised. 'It's a great song,' he said. 'I gave it another listen, and it really is.'

When Dicko came to Sydney one weekend, we met up at a café beneath the old Channel 10 offices. He said I should come up with a half-hour set that I could play, and that in a few weeks he'd come and listen to it in my bedroom, or wherever I wanted to perform. 'Use a loop pedal,' he said. 'That's all you need.'

I wanted to be Kurt Cobain, and I couldn't see him using a loop pedal, so I messaged a guy I went to highschool with and asked if he wanted to play drums in a band I was forming. I sent him the demos and he said he was keen. I went over to his apartment in the city on a Sunday and his dad greeted me at the door wearing a Hawaiian shirt and khaki shorts. It was just the two of them; when I had known the guy in school he lived in a big family house in the Hills District. The kind of house with staged photos on the wall and plates stacked neatly in the cupboards. Now it was just him and his dad—I never asked what happened with his mum.

His dad left to go for a walk. 'I'll leave you two to it,' he said as the door shut behind him.

The drum kit faced out the window, some twenty storeys up, towards Sydney Harbour, and I sat on a couch facing the drummer's back. I plugged my metallic green Stratocaster into the amp I had bought and started playing a song I had written called 'Love Bug'. He tapped his foot along to the riff and said he remembered listening to this one, then gave me eight bars before coming in. When I heard drums playing live for the first time to a song I had written, it shot through me. I could feel the kick drum in my sternum, and the crack of the snare rode along the curvature of my spine. *This is it*, I thought. *This is fucking it.* I started smiling to the drummer's back. After the song finished he turned around and he said he couldn't hear anything I was playing. 'How'd it sound for you?' he asked.

'Fucking great,' I said.

We rehearsed at his place once more, then had to stop because we got a few noise complaints. 'I came home one night really drunk and started drumming,' he said. 'I think that's probably why they're so sensitive.'

Dicko flew down from Brisbane to watch us play at a rehearsal studio in Alexandria. We ran through a few songs and he said they were good. Then he asked us to play a set list in an order he would choose. 'A.B.A.C., Regret, High in the Sky, A.A. Camp. Can you do it?'

'Sure,' I said, and we did just that.

After 'A.B.A.C.' he stopped us and said to me, 'Hey sunshine, we need to stop you looking down at that pedal board all the time.'

When we walked to the car, Dicko asked if I ever had any blow-outs with my voice. The drummer chimed in, 'Nah, never, he never does.'

I didn't do any vocal warm-ups, and had started smoking to try to rough my vocal cords up, but I'd never lost my voice.

'Geez, that's good,' Dicko said.

I desperately wanted us to be a three-piece but I couldn't find a bassist. Eventually a guy I'd played football with told me about his housemate's brother, Rich. Rich was interning at a record label at the time and working closely with the band

Sticky Fingers. I messaged him and asked if he played bass and he said he did. He was over in Europe at the time, but I sent him the demos and when he got back he turned up to a session and the first thing I thought was that he looked like Krist Novoselic from Nirvana. When I dropped the drummer home that night I said, 'I reckon he's our guy.'

The drummer agreed. 'Yeah, when he relaxed and started leaning back, he looked good.'

The three of us started rehearsing in an underground storage locker in Artarmon two or three nights a week. We played our songs twenty feet underground surrounded by the forgotten objects of people's lives. Our music rang out over the furniture and cardboard boxes that took refuge in these steel coffin pens.

We had pedestal fans in each corner of the room, and paint canvas zip-tied to the wire frame roof, and a rug hanging behind the drum kit.

After a few months of rehearsals we recorded our EP out at a studio in Windsor.

The drummer finished his parts early in the morning—in one take, not done to click—and started drinking straight after. While Rich played his parts I went upstairs and sat on my own. I knew my presence during recording made him uneasy. There was tension between Rich and I, mainly because I was unwilling to let go of the wheel, to let anyone else have a say. We disagreed on everything, from song arrangements, to social media use, to the eventual name of our band, and each of us would make what we considered small concessions to get larger victories. When we finally started playing gigs, he'd be checking his pedals, and making sure the volume of his mic was right, and I'd be rushing to get off the stage.

We finished the recording in two days, and on the car ride back to the city Dicko sat behind me suggesting The Stone Roses songs for us to play through the speakers in my car. 'I Wanna Be Adored', 'Waterfall', songs like that. We were passing under the Pennant Hills Road exit when he picked up a book that was behind my seat. It was called *Selfie*.

'What's this one about?' he asked.

'Narcissism. How obsessed everyone is with themselves in the social media age.'

I played up the punk stuff to Dicko, but it fitted with the deep-seated cynicism that was in my life at the time.

I dropped the guys off at Rich's and then took Dicko to his hotel before arranging to meet them all at a gig later that night. We were going to see a band called Planet. Rich was friends with the guys in the band—Matty, Tommy, Jimmy and Harry— and had been using Jimmy's Sunburst Fender bass during all of our rehearsals. Matty, their front man, was the younger brother of the guy who plays acoustic guitar in the DMA's, Johnny. The lead singer of the DMA's is another Tommy.

I walked downstairs and saw Dicko, Rich and the drummer standing in the crowd watching the opening act. That was when I saw Grace for the first time. She had long black hair and a very discernible widow's peak. I'd never seen anyone who looked like her before, and the guitar sat so comfortably in her hands.

When she walked past me after the show I asked for her number. I said I wanted to message her about 'music stuff'.

Dom's set finishes and the bouncer pushes us all downstairs. I've had three or four people ask me tonight when I'm playing my next gig. It's been more than a year now since I was last on stage and I don't really have the desire to go back out and play. Last night, I saw The Buoys play at the Oxford Art Factory, and usually after I see bands I go home and start writing songs in their genre. But I've stopped myself from doing that now. I think the next time I make music—if I make music—I want it to be me and no one else. I haven't figured that out yet. Maybe I never will.

We're huddled in the corner of the courtyard, and Mason, who was just playing bass, brings up the first night we met at the Courthouse in Newtown. 'I was reading the article about your delisting and there you were. I remember it, but I guess it would've been a bit of a sour night for you, actually.'

Dom then says, 'But that's what you wanted right? You wanted out?'

Eventually I say goodbye to everyone. Dom puts his cigarette out and gives me a hug. Grace and I walk through the pub to get into the back of a cab. On the way the owner stops me and asks how my brother is doing.

'Last time I saw him he was on top of a table here for Mad Monday. He had to go and get stitches after that!' We both laugh.

From the back seat of the cab I can see the spot where on that night three years ago I grabbed my drummer after he started talking to people he didn't know about the importance of nuclear families. I was in the pokies area drinking vodka Red Bulls—not gambling, just trying to get some respite— and he was out the back with Dicko. Dicko stormed out and sent me a text saying something like, 'I can't deal with this dickhead, I'm out.' Rich said the same thing to me and left too. I found the drummer out the back and took him across the road. I grabbed him by the collar of his shirt and said that he couldn't do this kind of shit because we were a band trying to make an image for ourselves and shit like this would hurt us. He pleaded his case and then jumped in the back of a taxi that came past and I did the same. There is now a pink neon sign glowing over where we stood which says, 'Coffee'.

The following morning Dicko called me and said he'd been staring at the ceiling feeling a terrible dread. 'We can part ways now, if you want, and I won't mind,' he said. 'But I can't keep working with that guy.'

I kicked the drummer out.

Not long after, we had our first song played on triple j. I sat in Rich's backyard in Newtown smoking a cigarette when it came on. Dicko called me straight after the song finished. 'How good was that!' he said as soon as I answered. 'Fucking hell, sunshine, it sounded great!' I could tell he meant it. He always told me how the music made his heart beat faster. But a few months later I parted ways with Dicko too. I was on the couch at Kieren's and Mark Holden was talking on *Sunrise* or the *Today Show*, one of those morning shows, and said that his advice to any young person working with Dicko would be: don't. I wasn't worried that Dicko would screw me over, I trusted him deeply; he was essentially my closest friend for the best part of a year, and I think we both saw elements of ourselves in each other. He'd been talking about contracts for months but never made me sign anything, he even set us up with a lawyer to go over the contract he finally did send through— some bigwig from Double Bay who represented international pop acts like 5 Seconds of Summer, when we hadn't even played a single set. I'm pretty sure the forty-five minutes with that lawyer cost more than the band ever made. We cut ties with Dicko because Rich and I were fighting for a certain kind of legitimacy, and we didn't think Dicko gave that to us. In a last-ditch effort, Dicko met us downstairs at the Lansdowne Hotel and offered to go halves in a record label with the band, saying he'd put up the money, and we could name it and sign other artists we liked and run the thing. But our minds were made up.

We ended up signing with the label Rich interned with. When we moved out of our storage locker, they let us use their rehearsal space a few times.

These days Rich is a successful talent manager and I think Dicko is still on the hunt for a young band to cleanse his defiant punk rocker soul from all those years in corporate music. And every six months or so I get a text from the drummer—sometimes about the songs we used to play together, sometimes about the songs I wrote after I kicked him out. The texts usually come in the early hours of the morning.

There have been other bands I've formed since then. Bands that I feel are always trying to rectify that original band's mistakes. But that band was my first, and was itself an attempt to rectify something else entirely.

OUT

Vince stood up the front of a meeting in 2016 and posed a riddle to the group: 'How far can you run into the woods?'

Without hesitation I answered, 'Halfway.'

He looked surprised that I'd got it so quick.

'Yep, and why's that?' he asked.

'Well,' I said, 'at some point you're no longer running into the woods, but out of them.'

JUST ONE OR TWO

It was Friday afternoon, the end of the second week of pre-season for the 2016 season.

I was dressed as a pink genie—long aerated parachute-style pants, a tight fitting crop top and a thin fabric veil on my head—watching on as a 6-foot-10 lizard wielding a staff made of VB cans kicked a hole in the side of a fibro plaster shed.

The house we were at was being rented by some of the new players at the club. It was down the road from Maroubra Junction, and the three bedrooms were still devoid of any personal possessions except for the suitcases they had brought in after draft night. This was a new house, one that hadn't previously been in the Housing Program, one whose lineage could not be traced back to former occupants now removed who only existed in our lives as call-backs in conversations.

The empty cans in the lizard's hand were stacked end-to-end and held together by grey electrical tape. His goal was to be the first of the group to make the staff equal to his height, because in doing so he would win the coveted blazer we had bought from Vinnies and embroidered the names of footy trip B.O.G.s and soon-to-be Wizards champions onto.

The backyard was a large open square and the neighbours peered in from their balconies, watching on stupefied as we each took turns at trying to uproot a palm tree by tackling it.

'My turn,' I said, and I dug my toes into the dirt and attempted, with as much effort as my drunken state would allow, to push the palm tree over with the force channelled through my shoulder. It was to no avail.

Our teammates cloaked themselves in bathrobes, fake beards and pointed hats. There was a Carlton Draught rubber bar mat on the ground which you were not to step on, and pointing was forbidden; elbows were to be used. Every time you took a drink you had to take an imaginary bird off your shoulder, then return it once the drink was finished. I had seven cans stacked in my hand and I walked around the side of the house to piss. I saw a boy wiping the vomit from his face with a Santa Claus beard. My piss trickled near him. I could taste vomit of my own and passionfruit in my mouth.

The game was Wizards, and it had been organised by me and guys like me. Guys who had been on the list for several years now and were unsure where we belonged. Who had lead the charge in pre-seasons gone by, and had ticked all the boxes of the running programs, but were thrown back and forth between seniors and reserves, all the while convincing ourselves that we were scapegoats. We were the guys who sat at the autograph table on signing day and slowly watched as more and more players moved to the other side of us each year because of the 'games played' seating order. 'Games played' was a trump card from which there was no return.

It was an unarguable truth which pushed you to the front of queues on photo days, and though said as a joke, it was lined with an element of truth that every player accepted, a continual reminder of your place and value.

We were the footballers you never hear about, torn between the outward extension of our personal trademarks and mantras which told us to keep going and never give in, and the reality of our talent and the fact that only twenty-two names were chosen each week. We found solace in each other and would will ourselves through to the end of the week by organising extravagant piss-ups on Friday afternoons, which we saw as opportunities to completely write ourselves off. In our Friday afternoon gym sessions we would be manic, screaming at each other, smirking, as our bodies prepared themselves to be burned down by the alcohol. Retired NBA basketball coach, the renowned Phil Jackson, once wrote that, 'The key to coaching was to keep the five or six guys who got little or no playing time from banding together and poisoning the minds of everyone else on the team.' We were those guys. As we drowned our sorrows we cried out, 'Fucking drink, you little virgin cunt!', 'Get naked, naked man!' and 'Come on, you little pissant!', though the harshness of the written word is an injustice—we were always laughing while we tore shreds off each other. We were thick-skinned journeymen crucial to the social fabric of the club. The ones who would turn the showers on in the morning so that the hot water was ready for our teammates, and, as the bridge between seniors and reserves, always knew where team dinners were each night. We'd been broken down for four years, and moulded into shape, and now it was our turn to whip the newcomers and show them how ruthless we could be—or at least provide a cautionary tale of where things might lead.

The night went on and eventually the winner taped the final beer to his staff, which I think was fourteen cans high. We made him stand still, his bathrobe barely clinging to his shoulders, and held the stack of cans against his back. The top of the highest can reached past the top of his skull and we all cheered. Then we got down on one knee and all yelled out, 'SPEECH, SPEECH!'

Instead, the winner laid his staff on the ground, lined up his feet so that the tips of his toes were parallel to the cans, and perfectly executed a hang clean Olympic lift over his head.

'That a fookin boy!' I yelled, imitating our new Irish strength coach. 'Get those hips through there, buddy boy!'

More boys finished their staffs and a wrestling match broke out, though the palm tree remained firmly in the ground. One of the boys, wearing a white bathrobe, walked out the front and got in his car and started to drive off. We chased him down and opened the door and pulled him out. We got changed and went to Coogee Pavilion and the guy who'd tried to drive his car threw his wallet into the open air from the third floor of the venue and hit it with his hand like a first serve in tennis. His cards spat out into the stairwell void and fluttered down to the ground level below.

In the locker room on Monday morning we reminisced and laughed about the night, and agreed to all pitch in $50 to cover the damages to the shed. Then when the whistle blew we were at each other's throats on the field.

The binding agent of my life had wilted and I started to live at emotional extremes. This is a recurring pattern in my life: all or nothing, black and white, love and hate, winning and losing.

Alcohol was a numbing agent, used to disolve myself every Friday night, and it sat at one end, counterbalanced by writing, which had become an act of permanence; capturing my fleeting thoughts and preserving them on a page.

When I wrote, I did so without any idea of what it would be used for. I didn't know any writers and had never heard about the pathways or careers that writing could lead to. My writing was a pursuit of nothing—a freedom.

I started carrying around cheap plastic-covered exercise books that I bought from the newsagency everywhere I went. I would name the books and then fill their pages with lyrics and poems—each was written with raw and brutish heavy-handedness; my handwriting often illegible in its erratic trajectory across the page. Throughout, common themes were clear: abandonment, loneliness, outsiderdom and the need to escape. I re-read them knowing the words were inspired by particular events, though in some cases those events could have been any number of things.

'Sleepless'

The soul speaks its
modest truths through the
dreams we surrender to each night.
The guilt and remorse of a
person reveal themselves

when no one else is there to judge.
For this reason I stand by
what I believe
when even in my dreams you
still treat me the same
and I wake in
cold sweat
dripping from my brow
knowing that the
fist I threw
was direct and true.

'Coat Hanger'

You're back in town
for what I assume
is only a brief stay.
Then it's off to London
or New York.
Paris, Tokyo, Berlin.
Wherever they choose to send you next.
From what I can see
you haven't changed a bit.
You still cover those freckles
and worry that the
tape will tell you a number you
don't want to hear.
For months we fought
through conversations of six

or seven words,
but now that you're back
I wouldn't mind a word or two so
we can reminisce about
that first night in your seven XL
white tee,
and how we made love in my friend's
sister's room under a collection of
her holiday photos,
or the time where you ran
to the bathroom because I was too stubborn
to open my mouth,
or the time I walked away without notice
and got a taxi home
only to wake up to your lips the next
morning.

I had to leave
briefly
to throw up the red wine.

'The Birch Tree'

Out of fire,
dirt,
ash,
and anything that should
cause a thing not to
be;

the birch does just that.
And it does not grow
with a crooked spine
or the need for pity.
It grows head to the
sky
with a strength that
endures.
Then, once grown, it does not
sprout legs and walk away.
It is firmly rooted in the soil from which it is made,
etching itself towards
the sky above.

———

We had rules about our drinking.

In pre-season we trained Monday to Friday and were only allowed to drink once on the weekends—we usually decided this would be Friday afternoon, so that we had the longest time to recover before Monday. In-season, the rule was that there had to be seven days between games for you to have a drink. When you put those rules in the hands of guys who were disgruntled and felt underappreciated, you got an abuse of the system, a pushing to the nth degree in an attempt to undermine authority. I am not an alcoholic; I don't need alcohol to live day to day, but I have been a binge drinker for most of my adult life. One drink is rarely one drink. I approach drinking with the same all-or-nothing ferocity as a pre-season training session. Drinking is a race; a test; a challenge to see how fast I can get to the point where I shouldn't be able to stand, and then I try to have one more. There is nothing elegant or sexy or suave about a binge. It is an ugly mess; a purposeful destruction.

Two weeks after our game of Wizards, we walked down Oxford Street with golf gloves on our hands and custom-made Paddington Open scorecards in our back pockets. It was the middle of the day and we had mapped out a route of eighteen pubs that made up our Saturday morning pub crawl course.

We planned to spend half an hour at each venue; the premise was that each pub was given a certain par score, where a par two meant you had to have two drinks within the half-hour to break even. As such, three drinks was a birdie, one drink was one over par. Basically the winner was whoever consumed the most alcohol by the end.

I started with three birdies—nine drinks in ninety minutes. Deano, who I was living with at the time in a place on Frenchmans Road, and who was in a similar playing situation to me, saw that I was surging ahead and started matching me drink for drink. We started going back and forth at each other. Whenever I got drunk I used to push Deano's buttons. At our house-warming the week before I'd thrown his patio furniture off our balcony onto the road three storeys below. I was in the midst of a very destructive phase, always breaking things, including throwing chairs off high places that chairs shouldn't be thrown from, like off the top of boats into Sydney Harbour.

After the fourth pub we stopped off at Kieren's house for a golf chipping contest into the water fountain in his backyard, and then made an impromptu visit to the house of Lewis Roberts-Thomson's parents which was across the road from Kieren's.

Deano and I were still going drink for drink when we reached the seventh hole. At the seventh you could drink whatever you wanted—up to that point it had to be beer or cider only. I opted for vodka sodas because they were the fastest to down.

I walked up to the bar and ordered eight. The bartender poured the drinks into short glasses and placed them on two round black carry trays for me, I think assuming they were part of a round. While standing at the bar I used my hand to scoop out the ice from the glasses, which I threw on the floor of the pub, and then I started to down the drinks. Eight drinks would put me way in front. Deano saw what I was doing and ordered a round of vodka sodas too.

After five or so had been downed, a waitress stood in front of me with a tray full of brightly coloured shots. She waited for me to move, but instead I reached out and stole one and drank it in front of her. Deano told me he saw it happening. 'Mate,' he said the morning after, 'I could see your mind trying to process who the drinks were for and then just going, *Well, there's no one else here so they must be for me.*'

The waitress wasn't impressed, and she called out to the bouncer who made his way towards me. 'Kick him out,' she said frustratedly, before walking off with the rest of the shots.

The bouncer puffed out his chest and said, 'Get out of here, mate.'

I replied, 'Fuck off, I didn't even—' before he started pushing me in the direction of the door. As he did, the boys started to sing me my farewell song.

It was bright outside. Sunny. No later than three in the afternoon. I stumbled towards a wooden park bench in the middle of Five Ways Paddington and lay down. I put the soles of my feet on the bench and shut my eyes.

I woke the next morning at home with the scorecard stuck to my face. The seventh hole had an array of lead pencil lines next to it, each more erratic, frail and further away than the last.

My head felt like concrete and I looked for my phone and wallet but couldn't find them. I walked into Dean's room and asked to borrow his phone so I could call the last pub we were at to see if anyone had handed in my phone. 'Oh yeah, and who won?' I asked him.

I can't remember who he said, but their name is on the jacket somewhere.

That night I had dinner with Kieren, who had heard about my night from some of the other players who had found me on the park bench and dropped me home. We were sitting at his dining table, and on the fireplace behind him I could see a framed photo of me and him from my first game with the Swans. In the photo he's got his hand on the top of my head.

I knew he was going to ask me something about my drinking.

'So . . . do you ever just have a quiet drink? Like just one or two?' he asked, hoping for some ounce of sensibility from me so he could have peace of mind.

I looked not at him but at the TV and said, 'What's the point in that?'

He didn't know what to say back, so I added something like, 'It's okay, I'm fine, I know my limit.'

That Friday we didn't organise an event but we still had our usual Friday drinks.

About a month later I got a phone call saying I'd returned a positive hair test for cocaine. A psychologist got in touch to talk to me about it. I denied ever touching any drugs. 'This is going to be a waste of both our times,' I said. 'I know drugs are bad; I must've picked up someone else's drink or something, that's all there is to it.'

I didn't have to do any counselling sessions. Though looking back now, I wish I had.

THE 27 CLUB

We like stories that make sense. We like things that fit into schemas. We crave clarity; we justify the present as an extension of the past; we attempt to reconcile *truth* and *order* when confronted with chaos. We yearn for the hero's journey and run towards stereotypes and character tropes, forever seeking resolution and progress. In all that we do we seek a finish line that justifies the journey, even though the truth is that in many cases these things do not exist.

For the first twenty-one years of my life I held this idea of what it meant to be a footballer—even if I wasn't sure it was what I wanted. Still, I thought that maybe one day the fulfilment of *the footballing dream* would justify my existence. After three years in a professional environment, I felt like I was holding the rotting carcass of football in my hands. I didn't enjoy the game and I was so aware of the pain it had caused to the people around me and myself. I was living a narrative that I didn't understand, so I tried to replace it with another, and I ran away into a new identity that I constructed.

I saw that the furthest I could go from being a professional athlete was to become some iteration of the tortured artist. I became a nihilist convinced that artistry was my salvation; that emotional pain—as opposed to physical pain—was my calling. I thought that everything was fake, and that the role of the artist was to see this, and live burdened by the truth. I became an antagonist to happiness and saw anyone who was happy as ignorant to the truth that I now knew—that life was filled with meaningless pain.

I drew a line between football and my new creative pursuits and saw that moving towards one was the escape from the other.

———

I was oddly comforted by the fact that I'd only played twenty-seven games, because twenty-seven is a famous number—one of prematurity, where talent had been wasted. Kurt Cobain. Janis Joplin. Jimi Hendrix. Amy Winehouse. Jean-Michel Basquiat. They all died at the age of twenty-seven, and forever since over them has hung a big ethereal cloud of *if*. There was both a finality and an unknowingness to the number twenty-seven, and the more I thought about it the further I became removed from the sense of failure I felt in my life. Those twenty-seven games made me feel like it wasn't that I was not good enough, but that I just didn't care enough. So at the start of my fourth season, with a 27 next to my name, I decided that I didn't want to play any more senior football, instead being content to ride out the next two years of my contract.

I trained as a pure midfielder. I did this for two reasons. First, it meant I most likely wouldn't play seniors unless there was a string of injuries. Our midfield was Joey, Kieren, Hanners, Parks and Tom Mitchell. Then on the cusp were Isaac Heeney, Jake Lloyd and Callum Mills; the latter two ended up playing in the backline, such was the strength of the group at the time. Even still, I had my moments. In our first intraclub game at Henson Park I kicked three goals in forty minutes and was the best player on the field, but for most of pre-season I floated like a ghost through the hallways of the club and attempted to take the yellow bib whenever I could at training.

A sign of my resignation came at the end of pre-season when we again did that exercise of the naming of the best twenty-two. I remember Zak Jones fighting his case, demanding that he be picked in the team even though he was injured. My name was off to the side like it had been the year before, but I didn't raise my hand this time around. First-year player Sam Murray did though, on my behalf.

'Why isn't BJ in any of the teams?' he asked.

Bud, sitting towards the back right of the room, replied, 'Well, in the few months that Paps has been here I think he has already shown more.'

I was given the right of reply, but I just nodded my head.

Second, playing midfield meant that I could stat up in the reserves. When games started, all I cared about was being able to walk into the development office on Monday morning to see the number 30 in the disposal column of the stat sheet next to my name. It was a part of my new *Good Will Hunting* mechanism; my way of saying that I was burdened by this *gift* that I had and that I now didn't want. I could puff my chest out and have everyone tell me that I should be in the team, even though I didn't deserve it. I wanted to be in the 'fuck you' position, but I didn't want the opportunity to prove that I was right because if I finally got the chance to play I knew I would be exposed for the cheap player I had become: a player who didn't run defensively, who cheated forward, who sat at the front of stoppages and rarely came off the field.

I had completely disassociated from the on-field expectations and I became detached from everything else at the club too. I avoided going to see the coaches for feedback; I had an arrangement with Shawry where we wouldn't review my games unless he had something urgent to show me. In 18 vs 18 I'd get a rise out of ruining the drill for seniors by getting clearances, intercepts and kicking goals against them. We—the reserves players—tended to carry on a bit when those things happened. If we got a run-on, Horse or Dewy would throw the ball up at the stoppage and yell out 'RED FOOTY' or give a free kick to the senior ruckman. I stopped doing the seniors' homework—though I made James Rose put my number on his sheet of paper a few times to make it look like I was still somewhat invested—and I stopped attending senior games. If us reserves had played out at Blacktown in the morning I would drive straight past the SCG on the way home, stop off at a drive-thru bottle shop on Anzac Parade and get a ten pack of UDLs or ciders, go home, and start drinking. If I had a matchday appearance scheduled at half-time of the seniors match—a signing session or an interview—then I'd try to swap with a teammate, and if that wasn't possible, I'd go and do it, then walk through Fox Studios straight after and drive back home. A few times people at

P.J. Gallagher's recognised me and called out, 'Jack! Where are you going?'

And I'd reply, 'Just putting my boots away.'

When the games were on I'd sit at home drinking with music blaring in the background—The Stooges, The Ramones, The Sex Pistols, The Clash, The Velvet Underground—and I'd plug my guitar into my amp and start writing songs. I'd text some of the rookie-listed players who weren't a chance of playing seniors and organise to go out that night; in 2016 it was to either El Topo or Pontoon. Before getting in the Uber I'd scroll through the stats from the seniors' game so I knew roughly how we'd played. I became adept at fabricating a story based off the numbers which would keep me in the loop at recovery the next morning or in the meeting on Monday. If our inside mids didn't have 25+ possessions each, then I'd be able to say we were beaten inside and were soft at the contest. If the opposition had a forward kick a bag of goals, I'd say our defenders weren't getting enough help. If our forwards weren't kicking goals, I'd say they weren't working together or that we didn't lock the ball inside 50 with our pressure.

———

Two months into the season I was given the chance to play seniors.

We were set to face Richmond, and I think Josh Kennedy— who never missed games—was under an injury cloud. We trained on the Thursday night, and at the end of the session I rolled my ankle in an entries-to-forwards drill. At our team dinner straight after, I sat with a bag of crushed ice on top of my foot which I kept elevated on a white plastic chair.

The coaches were all asking me how it was, and I'd lift the bag of ice and show them.

The next morning I went to get a scan before the team flight. When I woke up my ankle felt fine. I knew I could play on it.

At the clinic I had to fill out a form attached to a clipboard by a steel clip, circling where the injury was, and then I put on the blue gown and was given a pair of headphones by the machine operator. When I sat in the MRI machine all I could think about was how I wanted to be at home that weekend playing guitar and writing. I didn't want to travel down to Melbourne to play, because game day was a day filled with hours that I couldn't get back.

I couldn't keep still in the MRI machine, and had to redo the last few scans.

'Alright,' said the voice through my headphones. 'We'll have to do that one again, just make sure you stay still for this last bit.'

The machine sounded like a jackhammer.

Horse called me when I was walking back to my car.

'How's it feel, BJ?'

I figure most players wouldn't dream of saying no to playing a game of senior football, but when Horse asked me how I felt, I lied and said, 'It's no good.'

I lied about the injury so I could stay home. I lied about it because I knew it would show that the thirty touches I was getting each week meant nothing. I lied because it would destroy the construct I had created. I'd spent months cultivating a personal environment of angst and animosity and heartache, wallowing in pain from a chasm between myself and the world in which I lived. I was trying to torture myself. Partly as an escape, and partly because it's what I felt I deserved.

Whereas 27 was wasted potential, 28 would be *just not good enough*.

I hung up the phone and drove home.

Seniors played Richmond and lost by a goal after the siren.

SCARS

I have a scar just above my right wrist. It curves its way between the veins that run down my forearm, and is enclosed by sixteen dots where the stitches that tied my skin back together were thread. When I move the ring finger of my right hand a lump beneath the scar moves up and down. The lump was meant to go away, but never has. No one's ever asked me about the scar, though sometimes I see people staring at it when I hold one of the overhead tethers on a bus or have it resting on a table at a café. I figure this is because the scar looks like it is from a form of self-harm, and such things are taboo in general conversation.

The scar is from my childhood. When I was thirteen I chased Rhys across our front lawn after he stole a five-dollar note from my grasp that Kieren had just given me. When Rhys ran inside our house he slammed the front door, and I did not stop. I braced for the impact with my arm and it went straight through the windowpane which started three-quarters of the way up the white door. The shatter of the thick glass made a thundering, cracking sound. When I pulled my arm back through the hole where the glass used to be I saw white tendons staring back at me inside a large gaping hole in my arm and I screamed. It was a bloodcurdling scream. I flayed my arm around and dark red blood spattered across the wooden floor beneath Dad's jerseys on the entrance-way walls. My father ran from the kitchen; I remember the sound of his flat broad feet thudding the floorboards below. He looked at my arm and clamped down on the open wound with his hand to stop the bleeding and then we drove to the hospital. In the emergency ward they poured cold water over the area and it made me cry in agony. After surgery, the doctors said I was lucky not to have permanent nerve damage in my right arm.

My father has a similar scar, a bit higher up, more on the underside of his forearm. It is faded white, celluloid. When I was a kid he sometimes said it was from a shark bite, and other times a stick that flew up from the ground and struck him. In games he wore a large brace over it, which later sat somewhere in our house with the rest of the memorabilia. The day after I had surgery he and I made a game out of rolling a white stress ball along the slick sterile floor of the hospital, trying to get it to stop before a certain line at each end. That was thirteen years ago now. The scar on my arm is still very pink, though the top half is slowly fading to white.

———

I once had a taxi driver tell me that he and his wife had slept side by side every night for twenty-five years, and that he couldn't imagine falling asleep without her. My reply to that was that I could never sleep next to anyone, that if I were ever in a serious relationship, or even married—which I did not see as likely—then we would have to have separate beds. The cabbie laughed. I was twenty-one at the time.

Whenever I've told somebody that I love them, I've cried.

The first time I ever told somebody outside my family, I couldn't even say it out loud, so I wrote it down on a piece of paper and handed it to them. When I do say it, I feel my jaw stiffen and my eyes well, and the silence that lands after the words feels like it will entrap me forever. I cry because it is a nakedness for me, an openness that I find discomfort in, one that requires me to push to a point that I rarely reach.

I played a Swans reserves game at Blacktown in 2016. It was a cloudy day and there was fog on the field when we arrived. By the time the game started there was a handful of people scattered as our crowd. Between each goal there was a deafening silence; we won, I think.

After the game I sat at my locker in the changeroom. I was tired, heavy—narcotised almost, as that's always how my body feels after games. My mind still runs but my body feels battered, feels worn and present. I find solace in the destruction that has taken place.

I gingerly took off my boots and socks and started to rip the tape from my ankles. Then I heard a familiar voice, one I had not heard for some time.

When I looked up I saw my father, wearing a zipped-up fleece jacket, standing in the doorway of the changeroom. He was shaking hands with some of my teammates. Beside me someone said, 'BJ, is that your old man?'

'Yeah,' I said. 'What the fuck's he doing here.'

I watched Dad make his way around the room before finally standing in front of me.

'Hey Brandon,' he said with a smile that I've always felt said, *Let's just pretend* . . .

I was tired of pretending.

———

I remember one time I fell down the dirt hill behind the soccer goals at Edward Bennett Park. I was with Dad and he said that I could've broken my legs except that I didn't because I knew how to fall because I was a footballer. I had dirt and thin red scratches on my knees and arms, and when we went home I ran up to Mum and said, 'Dad said I know how to fall because I'm a footballer.'

My father dropped out of school in Year 10 to work at the steel mill in Figtree because that's just what you did where he grew up. If he'd never played professional football then I think he would've spent most his life in the mill and he would've probably stayed down around Wollongong and I doubt he and my mother would've ever crossed paths. But he did play football, and he was a good footballer, a great footballer, one of the best footballers in the world for a period of time. He did almost everything one could hope for in a career and then after football he had a sports store, and coached, and kicked high balls to three young boys who all hoped to be the Australian fullback one day. Eventually he became a real estate agent, bouncing around between different agencies in the west of Sydney where his bosses were always thirty-somethings with collared shirts and perfect white smiles and names like Jason and Mark. After real estate he worked in commercial flooring, and now I think he is a rep for TAB.

My childhood memories of my father are not of him as the mercurial deity who fans on the hillside of Leichhardt Oval in the eighties knew. What I saw was a man searching for a life outside football—a budding entrepreneur who kept a copy of *Chicken Soup for the Soul* on his bedside dresser; who chipped golf balls across the road from the base of our letterbox every night. A man whose Nokia slide phone rang out with 'Clocks' by Coldplay as he negotiated sales of Blacktown properties to put a roof over our heads.

I used to wonder why so many retired players flocked to commentary boxes and the coaching ranks or back to local football, but now I realise it's not because they cannot do anything else, but because they do not wish to look elsewhere and cannot let go—not of the fame or the spotlight, but of the game to which they have devoted themselves. My own re-entry to the Real World was one I had looked forward to for some time, but upon my descent I did not expect to miss the Footballing World as much as I have. To live with the mountain peak in the rear-view mirror at a relatively young age frames life in a backwards way that few people experience. Maybe this is why trophies are kept, reunions are held, and jerseys are hung.

Dad wasn't very handy, didn't know much about cars, wasn't blessed with the gift of the gab, but he could play football bloody well, and in our world, excelling at football makes you important—to clubs, to fans, to communities. Dad could run at a defensive line at a breakneck speed that few others would dare to reach, and he was respected for it, respect that I do feel he deserved and had the right to be proud of.

Because of football, because of professional sport, there is always an immediate connection drawn between my father and me. Even though we played different codes, people say I have football in my blood—that I was born to be a footballer. But what does blood know of games with man-made rules? As with anything, blood is only ever part of the story.

I have not had a relationship with my parents for almost seven years now. The how, the why, the when of any final inciting incident are minor details: Christmas Day, 2014, a passing comment by my father when it was just him and me. *His house, his rules*, something small like that, said jokingly. I took my bag, slammed the front door and drove away. My mother called me as I turned onto the M2 and I did not answer. To this day I've never been back to the house where I grew up.

Initially, I did not know why I reacted so strongly that day, but now I see that the moment was a culmination of something that had been simmering down below for many years.

The simmer that became a rift is now a divide that does not heal for many reasons.

Whenever I am asked how they are—and I can tell when it is coming up in conversation; if you have an estranged relationship with your parents you can always feel it circling around and you learn to think three or four sentences ahead—I say something like, 'They're good,' and then try to change the subject because I do not like to delve into a situation which I cannot reconcile and I do not want the discomfort I feel to be shared by those I am with. But perhaps right now there is something to the fracturing of our relationship that will help me find what it is I am after, and in that there may be some residual comfort for another out there living in uncertainty.

———

In the changerooms, Dad's outstretched hand hung in the air, waiting for me.

I looked at it, his crooked finger jolting out to the side. The same hand which had laced those boots on my feet after school all those years ago.

I did not meet his grip. Instead I stood up and said, 'Come with me.'

It had been over a year since we had last spoken.

He followed me out the door, into the car park, and I looked around for an empty piece of bitumen. I walked around the corner of the grandstand so that the roof sheltered us from the rain that had started to fall.

He tried to talk to me calmly, his palms facing outward, wearing an expression of trust and harmlessness. His words were an attempt to move our situation forward, but they harboured a forgetfulness.

I grabbed him by the throat with my left hand. My right clenched into a fist, trembling down by my side.

I told him to never come to my games again. I said that he wasn't a part of my life anymore. His eyes were glassed over in a way I'd never seen them before. He looked hurt; we both were.

When I instructed my father not to come to any of my games, or contact me, the words were deemed invalid, washed to the side, treated with the same scepticism as might be given to an unknowing child. Maybe all it would've taken to fix things was for him to say, 'Okay, I understand,' but that's probably naive of me and places the need to change on one side. I know too well that my father is not evil, or bad, but that he lacks a certain empathy and compassion. I'm sure, like many men before him, it comes as a result of the generational burdens he carries. With my own actions, perhaps I now carry the torch. But the knowing does not absolve him, nor me.

With my hand around my dad's throat I said it again: 'Do not ever come to my games. We aren't a part of each other's lives.'

My right hand continued to tremble in a clenched fist.

I let go and brushed past him, then went back into the changerooms, grabbed my boots and my bag and walked out without saying goodbye to any of my teammates. On the way to my car I walked past Mum. Her hair had less colour than I remembered, and she looked like she had been crying. She tried to grab me by the arm as I passed and she said, 'I love you.'

———

I am a combination of my parents. Kieren looks like Dad— in his running action, his tackling, the way suit jackets rest on his shoulders—Rhys like Mum, and I, with blond hair and brown eyes, a left foot and a right hand, am the middle ground.

Mum was the first person I called after Kieren and Horse told me I was making my debut for the Swans. That same moment, while I stood in the red-carpeted race that leads out to the SCG, I saw an orange paperclip on the ground. That orange paperclip sits in a tin can in my studio. It's the single piece of memorabilia I have kept from my years spent playing football.

It's very much a footballing trope to thank your parents when you win an award, and I've always noticed on Mother's Day TV footy specials, players always thank their mum because she took them to training and games or something along those lines. So often, mothers of footballers only get credit because they push themselves to the sides so that their kids can flourish. To be a caretaker is admirable, a role that some look forward to, though it's a flawed societal expectation of women to be caretakers, one that is exacerbated in the arena of football.

My mum was an only child; both of her parents' surnames ended with her. She was a registered nurse as well as being a mother who raised us and kept the house running. As I sit and write this, it's revealing to me how little I know about her. I know Dad's playing numbers inside and out; I know the stories of him burning dollar notes to the song 'Boys Light Up' after the Western Suburbs Magpies won the reserve grade Grand Final in 1981. I know the story of him stealing hotel beers during his round of a shout, and how he lost teeth tackling Mark Coyne, and how Paul Dunn shouldn't've let Wally Lewis get on his outside in Game 2 of the 1989 State of Origin series. But where in my canon are the stories and details about my mother's life? I do remember she told me once that before Dad she dated a man she referred to as 'the Canadian ice skater.' I know that she grew up on a farm in Mittagong, that her parents got divorced, and that for most of my childhood my mum's dad was not a presence in my life. I remember the way she would draw geometric patterns in black and blue ink on the back of envelopes while paying bills over the phone. I remember that when it was just the two of us at home there would be daytime soaps on the television screen. And I remember that there was a period when she wore a brown wig, which at night sat atop a Styrofoam mannequin head by the mirror in her bedroom, because she had lost her hair. Why, I never knew.

If I sit and think for long enough, more comes to mind: there was an artistic side to her family somewhere—the name *Rupert Bunny* was brought up once or twice with an air of pride. I remember her singing in the car and knitting in front of the television and I think as a child she had painted or drawn, and danced—her old ballet shoes were somewhere at home, buried beneath all the jerseys and boots. If I sit and think for long enough, the stories do come, just not as easily as they should.

My mother's existence seemed to be based around her husband, her boys and football. Driving us to training. Cooking us dinner. Cleaning our dirty shorts and socks. She'd married a footballer, and then she watched as her three boys had the chance to become footballers too. The thing is, I've never known if football is something she loves, or even loved, or even liked. Not once, throughout all the car trips to and from training and games did I ask her. Maybe if I had, I would've heard an answer that would make sense of my internal struggle.

Mum was the protector of our family. There was a fearlessness inside her that did not shy away from conflict, and it made me feel a hot flush of pricks along my arms and down the back of my neck whenever that fearlessness emerged.

At a game of Kieren's once, two drunk men exposed themselves to me on the field while I was kicking a ball on my own. I would've been ten at the time. When I told my mother what had happened, she paced across the field searching for the men. I was more concerned for their wellbeing than hers if she had found them. That relentlessness, or tenaciousness, or whatever you want to call it, was her way of protecting us and, I feel, of making herself known to a world which she was made to fit herself around.

Unlike my mother, I am a runner. I push people away, I go silent, I sleep on concrete stairs when there is a space in the bed, I cast people to Coventry. For years I would only share my feelings about my family on drunken nights out with strangers I did not really know. I remember I told one woman—her name was a colour—about my family on our first date. She asked to stay the night at my place; we slept back-to-back then she left in the morning without waking me. Usually I would be the one to leave. I'd say I had training, or a meeting, then go sit at a café on my own. Horse, and our player welfare manager Dennis Carroll, were very open and caring with me about my family situation, often calling me into their offices for chats, but I wouldn't allow myself to be fully exposed and I refused to show any hint of what I perceived to be weakness or vulnerability. I find it easy to fall back on the uncaring, disconnected, introvert trope; I convince myself it's an admirable form of self-reliance. I like to think I don't need anyone, that I'd be happiest on my own, but really inside I yearn for connection. Throughout my early twenties I would wake in the middle of the night reaching out for a partner who was not there. In my half-asleep state of consciousness I would be crushed to believe for a moment that the person I thought was sleeping next to me had grabbed their things and left.

My parents were my first source of love, but at some stage our relationship became conditional—bound by expectations at either end which when not met, pinned blame, and the deflating onus of disappointment. The thing about our situation is that it doesn't leave any scars on the outside, so it is difficult to know the extent of the damage, and it's hard to explain to people the toll it takes—which is why I tend not to. Even now I can't help but tell myself to get over it, that I'm wrong. At least with a scar I could look down and know for sure.

I have spent most of my adult life erecting barriers. Space is given and respected in bursts, but only ever as part of our cycle. A cycle which involves a hand extended, unmet, retracted, then raised in pain amid blame and guilt until silence resumes and the barriers are reinstated. Put simply, we are two sides wanting a version of the other that just isn't real. We both stand with our hands on a rope pulling in different directions, and even as I have grown tired and put the rope down to walk away in recent years, I still feel it being pulled.

———

That Christmas in 2014, I'd had five rings engraved with our surnames, which I gave to each member of my family. It was my attempt to say that the name 'Jack' was something worth keeping; circular rings are a sign of the eternal nature of love. I don't know where mine is now, but I know that my mother's sits inside an unopened express post bag that was sent to me one day. I have never opened the parcel, but I know the box is inside, and I know the ring is inside that box.

The idea that love is innate, that your shared blood entitles you to it, and is enough to substantiate it, is something that I have begun to question. And to believe that the word *love* is on its own truthful is a naivety. It is an easily thrown cover for other emotions, a justification for irrationality, and when taken blindly it becomes the love one knows, the love they feel they deserve, and their worth is obfuscated by it.

We often romanticise love as a selflessness; a complete loss of the self for another taken as its ultimate form. There are sacrifices and compromises, but the act of love is an ongoing commitment of work between two people, people who always exist independently of one another. Love to me is the ultimate act of give and take, of trust, of growth, of autonomy, and of life: it need not exist, but does. It may come. It may go. It will rise and fall and it will function alongside anger and pain, jealousy, sorrow and joy. That we may find others willing to work at it with us and that those people do not have to, but *do*, is more powerful to me than the idea of inherent love. Blood is thicker than water when we make it so; love at first sight will not last if it is reliant upon that first moment; and soulmates are not made by the intersection of fate alone. While the feeling of love is ethereal, the work required to maintain it is of this world.

Of my own experiences with love, I know this: to give in the expectation of return is less a love for somebody else, and more a fear for the self. A fear of loneliness. A fear of the incomplete. A fear hoping that somebody or something else will fix what is not theirs to fix. We can squeeze another's hand, and hope for them to squeeze back, but we should do so knowing they do not have to. Expectation, entitlement, whatever that version of *love* is, I know it deeply because it is the love I feel I have given to football my whole life.

I know that love can be cruel and that it may become our greatest source of pain. When love is unrequited; when one side asks to be let go and the other side wishes to hold on. It often defies rationality.

Heartbreak seems like one explainer of the current chasm between myself and football—but what were the foundations of this *love*?

There is a theory that suggests that the essence of trauma is a loss of the self. Exterior events, those are traumatic. But what happens to us on the inside, beyond the timeframe of any one incident: that is trauma.

Physician and world-renowned addiction expert Dr Gabor Maté says that in childhood, trauma may occur as we shape ourselves and suppress our authenticity to fulfil our need for attachment. A child will subdue the expression of itself—its screams, its outbursts, its desires—in order to receive affection and safety from its carers. Psychoanalyst Donald Winnicott provides a similar theory in his conception of the *false self*— he believed that emptiness in adulthood was a result of the creation of a façade in childhood.

The extension of this for Maté is that addiction is rooted in this trauma—addiction being any behaviour that a person finds temporary relief or pleasure in yet cannot give up despite the negative consequences—because it soothes the despair.

I've started to wonder if playing football was an addiction for me, or part of the disconnection I felt from myself. Perhaps it was both.

I am quite uncomfortable labelling events in my own life as traumatic, but when I look back I see a young man who sought the destruction of himself, and I can't ignore the kind of pain and silent suffering that one might usually associate with the word.

If I search for evidence within the years of my childhood, there are specific incidents that show a clear repression and curtailment of my personality in order to fit into a schematic, but beneath these lay a constant force that I have never questioned—one that taught me to shun care, weakness and difference. In doing so, I partook in the collective mutilation and cauterisation that many undertake to become the men we think we must be.

Within football I was given an identity, and I derived my earliest sense of joy from the fulfilment of that identity. I was validated by my parents, and would see them smile and cheer, and I would feel the warm comfort of family, so closely aligned to weekend games of football that the two became inseparable. When I re-read my old diaries, it's clear that the most bent I have ever been on football was when I felt the separation from my family approaching in 2014. Searching for love, I turned to the game and wrung the cloth dry.

Families are a dichotomy; the foremost struggle between individual and group. They exist in tension: a constant balancing of closeness and distance and freedom and loyalty. In their imperfections there are no definitive answers, and every family seeks common ground to unite them. Ours was football. Because no matter the space between us—the fights, the tears—we would still go and watch each other's games on the weekend, and talk about performances at the dinner table, and on that, more than anything else, we hung our conception of loyalty and family. That was our Church. Our weekly salvation. Our Sunday evening roast. Our board game night. Our way of family. Should football have been removed, I do not know what would have replaced it.

Like many parents, mine wanted their children to succeed in life. They encouraged us to play a game that we were good at, which they thought we enjoyed, and which gave us time together. Though I think they only ever saw the smile on my face, a smile that came because I felt they had smiled first. And because of that, the questions I now find myself asking were never asked back then. Instead, I grew up feeling three feet behind, constantly watching others and feeling enveloped by a blurred sensation. It's a distinct feeling which I still experience today, particularly in moments when there is nothing to anchor myself to; no pen and paper on the table, no guitar in my hands. In silence, which I do everything I can to avoid, the feeling intensifies.

Addiction. The inability to give up. So many times I wanted to quit, and I felt anxious just thinking about the game. Even now, the mere mention of a football makes the chemistry of my body shift in anticipation. After training and games, I felt tired, sore and mentally drained. I knew full well the physical and mental toll the game took and would continue to take on my body for years to come, but I could never find it in myself to say no. Even the moments when I did only lasted until the next session came around. In that sense, addiction is a common trait of athletes the world over; something drilled into the psyche for greatness. To be an elite athlete requires sacrifice and the commitment of time—which means life almost starts again when you are eventually finished on the field. But we push these things to the side, blinded in the pursuit of the elixir that only the games we play can provide.

Of all the drugs I have taken and the behaviours I have engaged in for respite over the years, none have gripped me quite like football.

For me, it was that thing so ever-present that it never felt like an expectation. There were no cones set up in the backyard and no forced early morning road runs when I was a child—but it was always there and over time became a vessel I could enter and feel safe; feel normalcy; an external expectation which seeped through my skin and became internal. So, while I cannot say that football is in my blood, I feel it has been made indistinguishable from that which does course through my veins.

I know there were moments of elation while I played—an indescribable euphoria from the movement of the ball, the tingling reverberation of my leg after a kick, and a sense of freedom and relief in the heat of the contest, perhaps exaggerated by floating in the stasis of my thoughts on either side of the game; and outside the lines of the field were the coffees between meetings, the games of basketball across the islands of the changeroom and the walks from the front of the club to the carpark at Fox Studios every afternoon—but like a drug high, what I cannot escape is the aftermath: the gnawing of my teeth and the staring at the ceiling. 'What is written about a person or event is frankly an interpretation,' wrote Sontag. That the high should not pour out of me onto the page as readily as it perhaps should speaks of something, something which may change in a year or two, or ten, but something which I feel now. On these pages is the evidence of the comedown that we don't often see, one that I am still very much in the midst of.

Hardly a day goes by where I don't search for meaning in my relationship with my parents, just as I do now with football. Both find themselves in the irresolute darkness of unmet expectations. Both lie at a point of ugliness we prefer to hide. Both I feel are unfairly burdened by my grievances with the other.

I stare up at the roof again and watch the fan spin.

———

Shortly after writing this chapter I went for a run with Deano around Centennial Park.

I wore casual New Balance sneakers because I do not own a pair of runners and I felt an anxiety far greater than a jog with a friend should incite, in part because I had not exercised in over a year. As we made our way around the dirt track it was clear that I still cannot run without trying to hurt myself. My version of running has never been for enjoyment, it has always been the pursuit of pain. To break myself down so that I can become something more. After the run, we had a kick, and Deano asked me to come and coach with him this year. The last year has been the only one in my life that I can remember without football. My last game was the 2019 AFL Sydney Grand Final, and the aftermath of that game was the point I realised I needed time away. I told Deano that if I do come back, it can't be a priority for me. No matter the pay, or the commitment they might ask of me, I know I'd end up thinking about it constantly. I need to take time away from the game so that it doesn't consume me again. He said he understood.

I'm sitting in my studio now, thinking that I'd like to at least try again, in a way that I have not done before, because while we ran and kicked I felt something that I have been missing of late.

BROTHER

Kieren came into my bedroom. I was facing away from the door, with the curtains drawn, towards the spot we had exchanged words the night before.

I knew it was him. I know how his feet sound when he walks, always bouncing on his toes with his heels never touching the ground.

That morning I had stood in front of my teammates and apologised. I had a black eye and there was a hole in the wall behind me caused by the rubber sole of my size eleven black Converse. My teammate beside me had bandages on his hand. After being driven home by the police for getting in an altercation outside a bar in Queenstown, he and I destroyed the Airbnb we were all staying at. When the rest of our teammates came home they started yelling at us.

'BJ,' my teammate whispered to me. 'I know how to fix this.' He ran into the kitchen and put his fist through the glass casing of the microwave. His hand split open, and blood went all over the mattresses on the ground. He was taken to the hospital to get stitched up.

Kieren lay on the bed next to me and started to pat my back. He was tentative.

He said he was sorry. His voice was shaky. He was the first one home to see the destruction we had caused. I was sitting in the spa out the back, and he came up to me and told me how selfish I'd been. He wasn't wrong. We exchanged words. Words which we now regretted. He was just a disappointed older brother trying to get through to a young man who wouldn't listen to anyone, who had become a destructive force to conceal the pain he felt.

I can always tell when Kieren wants to say things to me, and I think he can do the same with me. But we will never pry it out of each other. We will wait. That's what brothers tend to do, and sometimes they wait too long.

Our conversation started with footy. It's always been easier to start with footy for us; that's our language, our code, our common understanding. With my face still turned away from him, I said that I was thinking about leaving the Swans.

The back-end of the year was a write-off for me. I'd captained the reserves every week and we lost the Grand Final by a goal to the Giants out at Blacktown. We went to Home Bar in Darling Harbour after the game and I got a taxi home at 6.30am. For the rest of the season I still had to go to training to help make up the numbers in drills. Also, the strength and conditioning staff made us do some form of training on Saturday mornings, more as a way to make sure we didn't roll straight from Friday night into Saturday night than for fitness. One Saturday I was so hungover I couldn't stand for pre-training soccer, and so I just lay on my back on the artificial grass while the ball was kicked around me.

A few guys—mainly Deano and Toby Nankervis—were still in contention to play each week, so they had to prepare as usual, but the rest of us reserves players had free rein to have house parties during the week and nights out at the Sheaf, usually Wednesday, Friday and Saturday. I'd get through a deck of darts on each of those nights and for weeks after I'd wake up in the middle of the night having coughing fits.

Seniors made the Grand Final and so all us reserves boys met in the Virgin Lounge at Sydney Airport on Wednesday to fly down to Melbourne to watch. The day before the game we sat in AJ's backyard with slabs of UDLs and Cruisers and then went out to The Emerson that night. I had organised to meet a woman at the club who I'd been messaging on Instagram, but when she turned up she took one look at me and walked off. 'You were too fucked,' she said the next day.

I sat in the crowd at the Grand Final, very hungover from the night before. I had a couple of drinks during the game, but I was at that stage where alcohol tastes like the vomit from the night before. The seniors lost, and that night we went to The Emerson again. I got kicked out for jumping on the furniture upstairs, and then I threw up in the lobby of my hotel and the concierge took me to my room. I thanked him when checking out the following morning.

We all flew back to Sydney the next day and went to The Ivy and slowly got kicked out one by one. When I got home I destroyed my house. A chaotic spree which included smashing my favourite guitar against the wall and jumping on a table tennis table until it snapped in half. Furniture was flipped, glass was broken. Deano and I hired professional cleaners and plasterers to come in and fix the place up.

To Mad Monday I wore a dress, which eventually the team passed around and took turns wearing. We got kicked out after someone stole a bottle of tequila and climbed through the bathroom window and started drinking it.

I didn't have an end-of-year review meeting with the coaches. Horse just said he was happy for me to explore my options elsewhere.

———

Right before my first AFL game, I was looking around for my jumper in the changeroom. Kieren saw my frantic movements and told me not to worry. Then, in the coaches' room, I saw him standing up the front with my jumper in his grasp. He presented me with it and we hugged. A few weeks later, he ran through the middle of the MCG and kicked inside 50. The ball dribbled along the ground, then bounced up into my hands and I kicked my first goal in the AFL. As I celebrated, he ran over and rustled my hair with his hand.

I don't remember much of Kieren growing up. He moved out of home when I was eleven to play for the Swans and for the seven years after that we saw each other once every couple of weeks, usually after his footy games. I always counted down the days until I'd see him next, and looked forward to the end of the football season when he'd come home with a full travel bag and stay with us for a few weeks. There was a week in 2009 where he and I went to the driving range four nights in a row, and I remember leaving school those afternoons hoping that we'd go again, every day.

We both have a left-foot kick and carry the ball in a way that makes us look like we don't belong on an Aussie rules field. We were league boys from Sydney, who said jersey not guernsey, and semi not prelim. We spent our childhood mornings playing tackle bullrush on the bitumen of our rugby-union-dominated high school. Aussie rules wasn't meant to be our game. The code war rift did not allow for change, but Kieren did what no one else had done, and I, for a brief time, followed in his footsteps. I think my warped understanding of the game of footy stems from the fact that I had only ever watched him play before I got seriously into playing myself. So intently had I followed him that during my first game of Aussie rules I fell straight into a back-pocket tagging role. I didn't know anything else.

Kieren holds the record for most games played from the Swans rookie list: 256.

For his 200th game the Swans played Geelong, and I was flown down as an emergency. I wanted to ask Horse if I could present Kieren with his guernsey before that game, but I don't think I would've held it together. Macca did the honours instead. I sat up the back in my warm-up jacket and cried.

Before he ran out to play I hugged him and told him that I loved him. Before that, I couldn't remember the last time I'd said it to him, or anyone else for that matter.

He kicked the first goal of the game, and two more after that.

I ran down to the sheds after the game and we hugged once more. I clung tight to the back of his guernsey and he pulled me into the team huddle to sing the song with the boys.

28

When they lost the Grand Final that year to the Western Bulldogs, I walked across the MCG and sat on the ground next to Kieren. He was in tears.

'I really wanted that one,' he said with his hand covering his mouth and nose and his legs outstretched.

I pressed my shoulder closer to his.

'It's just football,' I said, knowing full well how impossible those words were to accept.

———

Kieren, like all other players, has his own relationship with the game of football. The same goes for his relationship with the Swans, the coaches we both shared, and the overlapping figures of our lives. Should he write a book, it would be different to mine, not only because our careers took different paths, but because we have different opinions, different beliefs, different interests. I know Kieren because I have spent much of my life trying to be Kieren, but there are parts of him that I will never understand, and parts of me that he will never understand either. A small example, one that I remind him of from time to time: he walked out of the movie *Joker* after half an hour, whereas I went back and saw the movie three times. Another: he is wise with investments, and finance, and money. Such things do not register with me. One more: he is good at small talk, whereas I fear two-storey elevator rides in hotels and apartment blocks.

I do not know if the loss of self I feel I have experienced also transpired in Kieren—from an outside perspective, I'd say it has not. I've always felt that the temperament I conned myself into came more readily to him. He showed the same conviction sliding across the carpet with ball in hand in those early VHS tapes as he did kicking his final goal on the SCG. But I know that we can never know the thoughts of others through observation alone.

I think it hurt Kieren to see my journey unfold and go the way it did. As a captain of the club when I was there, he would've sat in on a lot of match committee meetings where my name was moved off the whiteboard and from 2016 on he would've heard my name come up for consideration less and less. We'd get coffee once a week, and he'd always assure me that if I kept working hard then things would go my way. He saw part of the self-destruction, but never the full extent of it, and nor did anyone else because I cornered myself off from the world.

One of my biggest regrets from my footballing career is that I didn't play that game against Richmond in 2016.

I've always viewed it as the moment I turned my back on football, which I justified at the time because I thought it had turned its back on me. It's taken a few years, but I now see that it was more about me shutting myself off from those who were only trying to help—especially Kieren. All my games in the AFL, except for my last, were played alongside my brother. If I'd played that game, it would've been one more game together.

At a house party in 2016 a teammate said to me that he thought I should leave the Swans to play for another team. 'It'd be a good chance for you to establish yourself outside of your brother.'

'Yeah, you're right,' I said, but I didn't agree.

I was offered contracts by other clubs during my career, but I don't know how I would've gone on my own, and sometimes

I wonder what it would've been like at the Swans if Kieren had retired before I stopped playing. Empty, I suppose.

The truth is: what I really wanted wasn't to be a Swans player, or even an AFL player. I just wanted to play football with my older brother. Because right or wrong, *that was our way of family.*

———

After Queenstown I went to Airlie Beach for the week with a few boys, staying in a backpacker's hostel, before heading to a wedding on Hamilton Island. I was waiting for the ferry to the island with Tom Mitchell when he took the phone call from Horse that informed him he had been traded to Hawthorn.

When I returned to Sydney, I received my own phone call from Horse. He said that nothing had happened with me on the trade front, and that they were happy to have me back for another year.

When I hung up, Kieren called me on FaceTime. He was sitting in the park with Charlotte, who was crying. She held the back of her hand up to the camera. He had just proposed.

I hadn't seen Kieren that happy before. He told me that I'd be his best man.

Two years later he stood at the top of the wedding aisle in the Blue Mountains and I was next to him. When Charlotte stepped out of the car he started crying. The crowd turned towards her, and I took a step closer to him and put my hand on his back.

———

Recently I sat down with Kieren in Paddington for a drink. He's got a new job working in the city for a finance firm; to work he wears a button-up shirt and slacks. He asked how my book was coming along. I hadn't really told anyone what I was writing, but in my explanation to him, I said something about how we are so used to getting sports memoirs only from the guys who succeed, who have all the accolades, who get to ride off into the sunset, and I think we miss out on so much because of that.

'I had that career, the sunset one,' he said, 'and I still look back and think there are things I could've done differently. I don't think you ever retire without questions. I don't know if anyone's ever content.'

After a drink we walked back to his house, and there we started talking about football and the difficulty of transitioning out of the mindset we had held for so long. While we were talking, Charlotte reached up into the cupboard above the fridge and pulled out a small red pocket diary from 2003. She and Grace—who had joined us—read it in amazement. Kieren sat perched on a wooden bar stool, leaning over the kitchen counter, then turned his head to look at me.

'Flick to October,' I said. 'What's it say there?'

Charlotte turned through the pages. I could see manic black and blue ink scribblings firmly etched onto each page. Then she stopped.

'Oh, they're blank,' she said.

I laughed and so did Kieren.

'Of course they are,' I said.

Mine were always blank at that time of year too.

I'm now the age Kieren was when we first started playing professional footy together.

28

I was bent over at my locker, lacing up my boots, when Shawry crouched down in front of me.

Usually before games he'd give me a few focus points— something specific to work on or an instruction to give the rest of the team on the field. Things like, 'Make sure we are breaking on transition' or 'Don't let the mids collapse at the stoppage.' But this time he just put his hand on my shoulder and looked me in the eyes. 'I haven't given up on you yet. You can still play senior football.'

I didn't say anything back, I just nodded.

When he walked away, I slipped through a side door and went to the bathrooms in the empty changeroom next to ours. The sound of my studs on the tiles echoed, though no one else was around to hear but me. I sat on the floor in one of the shower cubicles, put my head between my knees, and cried. Air that felt like it had been forgotten, stuck deep in the pit of my stomach, came rushing up. I bellowed so much that I couldn't breathe.

It was my fifth year at the club, and I'd spent the entire pre-season as a small defender. When the full squad was back together we'd had a meeting at the Cricket Centre near the Sydney Football Stadium, and they projected our positional groups for the coming year on a large screen at the front. After playing midfield and forward for the past four years, I was now one of the six or seven pure defenders—a last-ditch attempt to find me a home on the field. From that moment I was moulded as the next Nick Smith. In a defender's meeting one day, Reg and Vince pulled me aside and said they thought I had what it took to be a great small defender after they'd shown clips to the defensive group of my repeat efforts and my ability to stick close to my opponent.

'I reckon your journey as a footballer will make you a great defender,' said Reg. 'There's fight in you, and I want to play with guys who know how it feels to have their back up against the wall.'

In our first intraclub game I played well. Shawry came up to me afterwards and said he thought I was one of the best players on the field. Then in a practice game at Coffs Harbour against North Melbourne I was given a quarter on Lindsay Thomas. As I was walking off the field Vince made his way towards me with a sight grimace on his face and said, 'Not your best stuff.' In my Monday review he said that I gave Thomas too much space. He pointed out stoppages where I was trying to catch him on the way through, and said I should've been in his pocket the whole time.

I was back in the reserves the following week. We played the Giants on Tom Wills Oval in Homebush. Dennis Carroll once made a comment to me that I was one of the guys who always wore their heart on their sleeve when I played, but on this day it was clear to anyone watching that my heart wasn't in it. This was around the same time that I'd started making music obsessively, and had been talking to potential managers, and had Dicko calling me three or four times a week to chat about making a band. I took the field that day, but I was elsewhere. I was drinking mid-week, living on my own, making songs till two in the morning. In the change-rooms after the game Shawry came up to me, and instead of giving me feedback he said we should get a coffee the next morning.

We sat at a table out the front near the road, and Shawry looked up at me from his coffee. 'So, what do you want to do next year?'

I remember choking up a little when Shawry asked me that question. I responded by telling him about my music and my writing. He sat and listened to me talk.

Then he asked, 'Well, what can I do this year to help? Do you want to sit in the back-pocket and play your role and have a chance at seniors, or do you want me to just play you in the midfield so you can enjoy yourself?'

The latter became the plan. After that I stopped going to defenders' meetings and slipped back into the midfield group.

———

Even during those times when I didn't care much about football, Shawry and I would still meet at the SCG on my day off and do a goalkicking session.

He'd wear his black-and-green size-nine Diadora boots—I think he was the last player to have a Diadora sponsorship—and wheel a bin of footballs to the Randwick end of the ground. We'd tip the footies out and he'd tie a large elastic band around my waist, then make me sprint with the ball in hand. He would grip the other end of the band and run behind me and as I was about to kick for goal he would pull the band and throw me off balance. If I'd held my form and steadied while kicking he'd cry out, 'GOOOOOD!' and I'd turn around and see his big white eyes bursting out of his shiny bald head in excitement.

There was an affinity between us—an understanding. He too was from a well-known footballing family, and there is an eerie similarity to our statistics from the first few years of our careers. He said he was shattered when I was dropped at the end of 2015. The game I missed was his last at the Swans. He went to the following Mad Monday dressed as Shane Watson, and I went as a cricket umpire—counter and all. With a beer in his hand, he told me to call him over the off-season whenever I wanted to go for a kick. A few days later I did, and from then on we met every Tuesday and Thursday at McKay Oval in Centennial Park. And yet those days were never about the ball flying between us.

When our seniors side lost the Grand Final in 2014, Rhyce walked to the front of the room and said with a very hoarse, almost inaudible voice that we couldn't let that game ruin us as a team, nor as individuals. He talked about his own experience at Collingwood after they lost the 2002 Grand Final.

'It took me too long to recover from that game,' he said. 'And it almost ruined me as a person.'

Maybe it takes something as disappointing as that to remind us that the game we play is just a game. Maybe we need to be almost completely ruined and have our hearts broken because the allure is so strong, so addictive, and the mindset so singular, that nothing else gets through. It seems excessive and unnecessary, but those who have been there will know. 'It's just a game,' we say, trying to convince ourselves of a truth we do not believe.

Regardless of my feelings towards football, through it I met people like Rhyce Shaw, and I would not trade our time together for a career, or an alternative life of any weight.

That day in the changerooms I stood up from the cold tiled floor, wiped the tears from my face, and re-joined my teammates.

———

I always knew that Rhyce would become a head coach somewhere, though I did fear the impact it would have on him. It's a brutal role, one with impossible allegiances: forty-odd individuals each have to be convinced that they should fit into a twenty-two-player team, and to resolve the resulting disgruntlements is a job too big for the one person who is often seen as the cause.

After one year of head coaching, Shawry had to take time away from the game. An old teammate of mine said they saw him the day after he had to delist ten or eleven guys, and they said that he told them it was one of the hardest days of his life.

Shawry's biggest asset is that he always puts people before the game, when most of modern professional football doesn't allow for that. So much of the ugliness of sport comes when people aren't the priority. When games become corporations, they broaden their appeal, provide avenues to heights not otherwise scalable for a select few, and create an alluring spectacle for wide-eyed fans, but in doing so they also run the risk of losing the profoundly luminous quality to which we are initially drawn. There are winners, and losers, but first and foremost football is a conduit between people; a means of connection; an opportunity to manifest that kindred spirit of belonging.

When news came out that Shawry was returning to the game as a development coach, I felt relieved. In an interview, he said, 'The experiences I've had throughout my career developing young footballers to reach their potential have given me the greatest satisfaction and pride, and I hope to have the opportunity to contribute to this great game again in the future.'

When I took the field after crying on the floor in the showers, I had something like 33 touches and a goal. Shawry named me best on ground. In the sheds after the game he gave me a hug.

'BJ, I've never seen you play like that before,' said one of my teammates in the showers.

We had a team meeting at Clovelly that Monday. Seniors were zero wins and five losses after making the Grand Final the year before. A sign that a football club is in crisis mode is when they start doing different things to the usual routine—like changing the scenery of meetings and training. The week prior, we'd played paintball instead of doing a game review;

here, we sat in a circle in the upstairs room of the surf life-saving club and one by one every player in the room was given feedback.

When it came to me, about halfway around the group, Horse said, 'BJ, how many games did you play last year?'

Without flinching I said, 'Zero.'

'You keep banging down the door,' he said, 'and at some point, we'll have no other option but to play you.'

The next day I walked out onto the SCG for training. While putting my GPS unit in my training jumper, Horse came and stood next to me. 'You're coming in for your brother this week,' he said.

That weekend I played my first senior game in over a year—game number 28, my final AFL game. When I stood out on the MCG before the game I was thinking about Shawry, and how I'd rather be playing reserves.

For a few years now I've said I wish I'd never played that game—I looked out of touch on the field, and didn't get near the ball. But now I think I'm glad that I played. Because it was for Shawry.

———

After I was dropped for the final time I spent the rest of that year playing reserves and mentally preparing myself for the end of my career. Before and after training, I'd kick torpedos from inside the centre square towards the goals at the Randwick end of the SCG. There's this moment with a torpedo, as the ball drops, when you hope it's going to go perfectly. The angled ball falls down, and you just hope. And then you know as soon as it hits your boot if it will or not.

I didn't ask my manager to negotiate with the Swans. When he asked if he should look at other clubs for me I told him not to bother. The reserves made the NEAFL Grand Final again, and we lost, again. By a goal. Again. If you're keeping count, this was my third NEAFL Grand Final loss in four years by less than a goal.

When the siren went I fell to the ground on the SCG and started sobbing. I was on my hands and knees with my face buried into the ground. I stuck my fingers into the dirt and ripped out some of the grass. Will Hayward sat next to me, and opposition players from the Brisbane Lions came up and said things like, 'You're a good player, Jack' and 'Hold your head up.'

When we watched the Lions team get their medals, a few of my teammates came up to me and apologised for losing the game. They felt like they had let me down. It was nice to know that they had been doing it for me.

I spent the next few weeks going to the Sheaf and World Bar, drinking and smoking darts. I knew what was coming. After our seniors were knocked out of the finals, we all went to Beach Road and I stayed at a woman's house in Bondi. During the year she had once come to mine, but left after I sat on the edge of the bed and told her I wanted to go out and drink with my mates. She picked up her things and slammed the door leading to the fire exit in my apartment block. I wrote a poem about it the following morning.

The morning after I stayed at hers, she drove me home. As I was about to get out of the car I got a call from a group of players who were still going from the night before. 'Oi!' they screamed. 'Get to Bondi now!'

She could hear them screaming and offered to drive me back to Bondi. I said she didn't have to, and that I felt bad about wasting her time, but she said it was alright.

When I walked into the backyard I saw one of my team-mates holding a glass of red and smoking a cigarette. Lying in the garden behind him was another teammate, shivering, wrapped in a blanket, gripping a bottle of Smirnoff vodka. I sat at the table, opened a carton of Winfield Reds and lit one up, then took a swig of vodka. There were only four of us there for a while until I sent a message to the whole team telling them to come to the backyard we were in. I said they should only come if they each brought a slab of Cruisers. I don't know why I said Cruisers, but by midday there were 40-odd slabs of Cruisers on the table in the backyard. The next morning, I saw that my exit meeting was scheduled for 12.20pm on Wednesday. Beneath it, there was a team meeting at 1.00pm. They always filled the hour before that final review with players heading towards a certain fate.

———

A few months ago I bumped into the woman who drove me to the house party that day.

'You never really struck me as a footballer,' she said. 'I could tell there was something else there.'

We talked for a bit, and I told her about the poem I had written after she had left my apartment earlier in the year. Part of it reads:

no goodbye kiss.
just your cold
untouched
peppermint tea on my table.

enjoy the ride home.
I hope you don't care
that much because
we never really got to
know each other anyway.

I'M SORRY

I sat in the chair next to the elevator looking into Dennis Carroll's office, hungover, awaiting a conversation I knew was coming.

I was alone, thinking about how as an eighteen-year-old I'd written out what I wanted from my football career, and how I put these slips of paper in a little wooden chest. I remembered writing down that I wanted to play 200 games, kick 150 goals, and be captain of the Sydney Swans. Five years later I had played 28 games and kicked 17 goals, and captained the Sydney Swans reserves grade team to back-to-back grand final losses.

Footsteps came down the hallway. 'BJ, you ready?' It was Horse.

I walked a few steps behind him, my right ankle clicking every time it lifted from the ground. When I walked into the War Room I saw Tom Harley sitting underneath the whiteboard on the wall. 'Have a seat, BJ,' he said.

The blinds were drawn and it was like being in a vacuum. An iPad on the table was recording the conversation, I think, or the thoughts between their last conversation and this one. When I looked at it Tom closed its cover and pushed it off to the side.

Horse started off. 'How are you, mate?'

I realised I was sitting in the exact same spot I had been when he told me I was going to be on the list, and the same spot as when Kieren told me I was making my debut for the club.

'I'm, ah . . . I'm good,' I said, a feign of laughter bookending the words that left my mouth. There was a resignation to my voice, a fading off at the end of the sentence. Not needing to add anything more, not trying to fight what was happening.

They both looked at me and we all knew what was going to be said. It didn't matter who said it, because the result would've been the same, but I wanted to at least feel like I was doing it on my terms, so I spoke.

I turned towards Horse, my right leg crossed over my left, hands resting on my calf. It was time to finally say the words I'd wrestled with for the best part of fifteen years. The words that I'd typed into my phone up in Brisbane, the words I'd wanted to say after the game at Leichhardt Oval, the words I'd thought about so much but never saw a possibility to say out loud. These words now sat on the tip of my tongue, and it felt like there was concrete on my face which I had to push them through.

'I'm . . .'

I feigned laughter again.

I'd seen this coming for the best part of a year. I'd joked about it a lot while on the piss, and in the showers after games,

but still, finally saying it out loud, and finally having it happen—
my throat became dry and my bottom lip began to shake.

'I'm . . . done.'

Breathe.

Horse leaned forward, his eyes wide open, his face soft.
I think he always understood me better than most. Maybe
because I was like many players he had seen before, or
maybe because beneath it all, he saw that I wasn't.

Out of all our conversations over the years, there's one that
meant more to me than any other. It occurred in my first week
at the club and had nothing to do with football.

He came over to me in the changerooms and asked how my
insulin pump worked. I pulled it from my pocket and showed
him, and while I don't think my explanation was anything
worth remembering, it was just nice to be asked about something like that.

I continued, 'I've done everything I can here, and . . . I'm
ready to move on.'

Horse nodded his head gently. 'BJ,' he said, 'I've said it
before but you're the kind of guy who can know that no matter
what, you left no stone unturned. And I mean that.'

I nodded and tried to contain the tears that were building,
my lids holding them back like a stormwater-drain grille.

I said a few more things. That I was excited to go to uni,
and to pursue music, and to write, and to find a life outside
football. Then after two or three minutes, I shook both their
hands and walked out of the room.

As I left I saw Shawry standing in the doorway of Horse's
office. I don't know if he planned this or not, though I'm sure
he would've known that the meetings were on.

I walked up to him and he pulled me into the room and shut the door. He looked at me with those big glaring eyes. We just stood with each other for a moment.

'I'm done,' I said. This time I couldn't stop the quivering. I let out that real heavy moan that sounds like it's your first time crying. Shawry pulled me in for a hug. My head burrowed into his shoulder. Seeing nothing but black was comforting. Then I started apologising. 'I'm sorry, I'm sorry,' I kept saying. 'I'm so fucking sorry, Rhyce. I'm sorry I couldn't kick, I'm fucking sorry.'

Shawry pulled back and put his hands on my shoulders. 'Mate, what are you sorry about? You did everything you could, I'm so bloody proud of you.'

We hugged again and then I wiped away the tears and walked down the hallway to where the rest of the boys were. I slipped into a conversation and told a few of them I was done, then they all went in for a team meeting and I walked down the stairs and got in my car which was parked out the front.

At the lights on Driver Avenue I called up one of the other guys who had been delisted and we went and got a coffee. I ordered what I usually would and there was a fly in the salt-shaker on our table.

When I got home I looked at my bank account and saw that I had saved $30,000 after five years. That money's all gone now.

In the three years since I retired from footy I've been in a few bands, fallen in love, and written three different book manuscripts. But right now is the first time I've really stopped to think about it all.

PART IV

SOUTH

I sit cross-legged while Grace and her sister Lily play the latest mix of their upcoming single over the speakers. The waves of Narrawallee beach crash in the background, and the distinct two-part sound of a whipbird draws and pops with predictable regularity. Hamish, their father, is out surf lifesaving, while their mother Tina sits with a book in her lap, harmonising underneath the vocal melodies of her two daughters.

———

Their house is a musical house. Guitar cases and amps stacked by the front entrance, an upright piano in the living area. A Maton acoustic guitar with flower stickers on it resting on a VOX AC30 amp next to the couch, a cigar box banjo beneath the TV and ukuleles hanging on the wall next to the fireplace. At any one moment, Grace or Lily or Tina or Hamish might sit at the piano and play. All sound good, though there are subtle differences in the weight with which their fingers move across the keys and the melodies towards which they gravitate. Without raising my head I can usually tell who is playing.

Last night we had a long table dinner on the back deck. There were ten people in total. Hamish's brothers are both visiting from America; it's the first time the three of them have been together in Australia for almost two decades.

'I always wanted to play it,' said Jack, the youngest, talking about the song 'Don't Bring Me Down' by ELO. 'But you guys never said yes.'

'Oh, you're kidding,' said Gus, the middle child. 'I can't believe we would've said no to this!'

Hamish, the eldest, sat pretending to play the drums at the other end of the table. Straight eights on the hi-hat, snare on the two and four. He stopped momentarily to mention how good the three-part harmonies were.

I find the three brothers to be slightly different versions of one another, though they all have the same giddy laugh and intent expression when they listen to you talk.

As the night went on they reminisced about gigs in Kings Cross and America, and their layovers in Scotland, and their old walk-on song—the orchestral finish of 'Mr Blue', also by ELO. I enjoy hearing stories about the band, and how Grace's family lived a bohemian life in America using beer boxes draped in fabric as furniture, and how the girls used to muck about inside two large refrigerator boxes and dress themselves in mish-mash outfits, and how Skunk Baxter from The Doobie Brothers used to give people a fake card and tell them he was in the FBI.

Before eating, we held hands and gave thanks for something from the day. Each person took a turn to speak while the rest listened. Grace's family has done this since she was a child, and now Grace and I do it at our meals together—not as a religious practice, but just because. It was strange to me at first, the holding of hands, the listening, the stillness, and the idea of something small being important, or that today can be good enough without the promise of tomorrow. I figure if I ever have kids, it'll be something I do with them.

After we ate, a bottle of whiskey—a favourite of David's, Grace's grandfather on her father's side—was brought to the table, and the night turned into a roundtable singing of old war songs. Songs which David and his wife Dawn sang to the boys and their sister Emily when they were kids, songs which Tina knows and sings too, and songs that Lily and Grace seem to recall through the lineage of those songs being sung to them as children.

When everyone was done with their meals, Grace and I stood up and collected their plates and started washing up. From inside, I could hear them all singing and laughing outside still. It was nice.

———

Grace and Lily's song finishes playing over the speakers. Tina stands and walks across the floorboards towards the next room, and on her way she tells her daughters how wonderful their song is.

THE ARTIST

'Art is never finished, only abandoned.'

Leonardo da Vinci apparently wrote that, though I can't find out where or when exactly, but enough people with credibility seem to attribute it to him for me to think the words were his.

It is, in some way, true of his most famous work, the *Mona Lisa*. Historians debate why the piece is said to be incomplete. One argument is that the artist loved it so much that he could never come to part with it; another, that the after-effects of a stroke rendered him unable to hold a palette or paint brush in the latter years of his life. Regardless, the painting of perhaps the most famous artwork in the world started in 1503, and is said to be have been abandoned—unfinished—by its creator who died in 1519.

Art and sport are often viewed as binary opposites, and I think this has something to do with the noise which brings a sporting event to a close. The finality of the siren kills creativity, for to be creative is to surpass structure and mechanism and absolutism; it is to be free. To be an artist is to float in space and never come down, and that ugly foghorn noise at the end of footy games roots players firmly in this world.

When the siren sounds, the game is abandoned and then buried, with the result etched on its tombstone saying who has won, and who has lost. One does not get this absolute with music, or painting, or the written word.

Two works can be placed alongside each other and one judged as better, though only by a subjective form of comparison, not the outcome of competition. The number one song on any music chart is the result of accumulated personal interest; not victory per se. There is not, and never will be, a definitive best song at any one moment, because in-built in us all are different tastes, a personal point-scoring system which cannot be universalised. All art lies on a spectrum of subjective good and subjective bad; while a song might win awards, it can never really *win* with absolute certainty. With no formal set of rules to crown a winner, the point scoring—appeal to taste— is done in a free and unconstrained manner. Creativity.

That is not to say that sport is devoid of subjectivity. Contention will always wage over who the best player is or was, and we do not all support the team that wins each year. Footy is rife with forms of emotional attachments which defy the logic of competition; still, at all times this exists alongside the absolute of sport: that there are winners and losers.

Competitiveness does not care for the how, it just wants to win. Creativity, on the other hand, is all about the how. It cares for the process. It seeks to entertain and evoke. It has no absolute at which to aim except for it to manifest itself.

The two seem like incongruent concepts, but athletes and artists do not sit at opposite ends of a spectrum. They are both dualisms, comprising the creative endeavour and competitive edge. The bulk of artists do not create to win awards or to earn fame. Selling out venues is a rarity; most are accepting of the fact that they won't make it out of the shitkicker venues at all. If you want wealth and notoriety then art is not the right career to pursue. Those who seek it will be weeded out fast by the lack of overnight success they crave. Most artists I know work stable(ish) jobs to earn money—there is a certain backroom at an Apple store in Broadway, Sydney, where they tend to gravitate—which they then pour into the sink of artistry, not expecting to see much of a return.

That is not to say that such people create for the sake of creating alone. They create art in forms and modes that stick to at least some conventions so that it can be seen or heard or read—so that it can be appreciated by others. In whatever form it takes, the art is often uploaded, and shared, and distributed; the artist seeks an audience even if that is just a few friends sitting around a laptop or Bluetooth speaker.

Even if their work is unshared, artists who refine their craft are competitive. With themselves, they compete in that they seek to be the best artist possible, and in every case they compete with reality, trying to bring something into existence which was not previously there.

Athletes do, however, seem to wear medals more naturally, and in the footballer's realisation of the absolute, competitiveness assumes a higher rank than creativity. If you ask a player what they want, it is usually to win.

But the football player is also a highly creative being. They make decision after decision on the field to create order from chaos. They kick when they could run, they run when they could kick; they float in the realm of artistry as their creativity comes from the pursuit of the outcome, rather than being destroyed by it.

Many view the brutishness of competitive and combative sports to be the antithesis of creativity. One is apparently of the body, and one is of the mind. One is high, one is low. One is central to the revelation of human truths, and the other is just a game. However, sport and at least the more conventionally acknowledged art forms are more alike than they are different. Both are born from positions of discomfort. I do not mean that in the dour sense of a tortured artist who sleeps on the floor, mending a broken heart, with a stomach filled only by narcotics, nor in the bloodthirstiness of the never-say-die athlete who pushes their body to the point of collapse. With art, the discomfort is more the urge to create something which does not exist. An urge that comes from standing at a point where you are not content with the current reality and seek to change something about it. *This song doesn't exist, but it must. These words must be written down. This canvas must be filled.* All are different iterations of the same drive to defeat the void of emptiness and impose oneself on the world.

Sport is built on the intentional creation of discomfort. The games we play consist entirely of putting obstacles in front of ourselves that needn't be there to make a somewhat simple task more difficult than it need be. For instance: kick a ball through those sticks, but you have to bounce said ball every fifteen metres, and the opposition can tackle you while you attempt do so. Without such obstacles sport would not be a test; it would lose its appeal; it would be forgotten.

Being abstracted from infinite possibilities, all forms of art walk a line between expectation and surprise. Even in the most predictable pop songs where you know the chorus is coming—because the song is constructed to guide you there through the repetition of a hook, following a predictable structure, and the resting on a chord which we feel must be resolved—the arrival still hits you unexpectedly, altering your reality in a way you weren't fully prepared for.

Music is the great con man of human consciousness, thriving on the battleground between familiarity and the unknown. Fiction does the same by occupying the middle ground between cognitive estrangement and verisimilitude. Should one dominate the other, a piece becomes mundane or incoherent, losing not only its integrity but the audience. Cliché—the ultimate form of predictability—is the enemy of a good story. So too is utter absurdity.

The writers of fiction split the difference—not literally, the balance can be tilted either way—and draw us into worlds we do not yet know while providing us with things that we do. We may be thrown into the depths of Middle Earth, but while there we witness characters who display values we know and follow plots based on the overcoming of obstacles we ourselves have experienced in some way, shape or form.

This tension—or harmony—between familiarity and uncertainty, between expectation and surprise, exists in excess amid the chaos of the grass oval canvas. We watch a game of football knowing that there will be a result, yet we are captivated by the possibilities which lie between the start and finish. A widely repeated fact is that there are more possible variations to a game of chess than there are atoms in the universe, yet we've seen the same game of chess unfold multiple times—though of course in such different styles and moods. We see the same final scores repeated in games of footy—but we will never see the same game repeated. Footy gives an absolute, while also harbouring a unique potentiality that anything could happen. How else could the irrational 'maybe this is our year' loyalty from supporters of perennially losing teams be explained?

A goal from the boundary is more interesting than a goal from in front, and a game that goes down to the wire is vastly more interesting because it holds off certainty for a little longer. Just watch the crowd walk up the aisles when they think they know the outcome of a game; something as menial as beating the traffic is more important than a foregone conclusion. The wrestle with uncertainty is what keeps us coming back.

Art—in the form of paintings, songs, poems, stories, etc.—is never finished, in that it can never become perfect or complete. There is always something more to add, and nothing to stop an artist from adding except for death. When I finished the first draft of the manuscript that eventually became this book, I kept a folder of notes in my phone and a notepad in my bag which I continually added ideas to.

This book could never have been finished if I sought to capture every single feeling I had, or followed every thought that came up pertaining to the work at hand. So, have I just abandoned it?

Finishing a work of art does not mean we must be utterly satisfied with what we have created, or that our feelings and thoughts will not change once it is out in the world. This is a feeling that football players know well, replaying contests in our heads the night after the game while staring at the ceiling.

'To finish' has an attachment to finality revolving around a state of absolute certainty, which most forms of art cannot attain, and to expect art to reach a point of absolutism is wrong, for art is the process between absolutes. The game of football, not the result after the siren, is the piece.

Art allows us to be happy in the presence of imperfection because it is not the aim: art is the expression of choices captured in time. Art is a continual sequence of stops and starts to form a whole. Where each expression ends is the artist's choice, and it is with choice that art can be finished.

Art that is unfinished in the absolute sense is not, however, abandoned. The act of abandonment carries a sense of helplessness—as though it is a forced response to circumstances which cannot be overcome; as though art is only ever abandoned because we are caught in a fight we cannot win.

I find it difficult to believe that each work of art is not in some way influenced by the one before it; one thought prompts another and lessons learned from failure inform the next stroke. An artist's entire life often consists of one continued piece which occupies different canvases.

It is before the final siren of death that the artist fulfils their role: to make choices which turn the uncertain chaos into a semblance of order, and to translate that which is not into something which is. They stand alongside the anarchy and unknown, and craft the infinite possibility into reality. They do not abandon.

UMA THURMAN'S EYES

I sit in my shoebox studio apartment above a family's garage in Paddington trying to figure it all out. The ceiling fan above my head is, as always, spinning. Its motion does nothing to make the room cooler, but it does disrupt the suffocating still-ness that has become my enemy. There is dust—or maybe mould, I can't quite tell—on each of the three twisted blades. I tilt my head back and fix my eyes on a point on one of the blades and watch it spin around and around and around.

The shower drips. I hope during each pause between the wasted water dropping into the drain below that it will be the last. *Drip*. Maybe this time. *Drip*. Or this time. *Drip*. Okay, this time for sure. *Drip*. I stand up and turn it off.

While in the bathroom I look at the flattened bristles of my toothbrush resting on the side of the basin. I brush my teeth with a fast aggression to remove the yellowing stains that have started to appear. I try to fit in two minutes of brushing in twenty seconds because I don't have time to stand in front of the mirror. Well, I do, but I don't. I should go to the dentist—one of my teeth is cracked, and I also need to get a filling, or two, or four—but my health insurance has a six-month waiting period and right now paying rent is more important. Anyway, I'm scared of the dentist, and if I go I figure I'll have to start by saying something like, 'Hey, please don't judge me . . .'

The garage door beneath me opens in a slow-motored waltz. My landlord is teaching his daughter how to drive. 'Go back, go back,' he barks. She reverses out and then adjusts the angle; I can hear the high-pitched squeak of the tyres on their garage floor. 'Now come forward. You'll be fine, trust me.' The front bumper of the black Mercedes nudges against the white plaster wall where my front door is. The engine turns off and they disappear into the backyard.

I walk out of the bathroom and resume my position on the couch. My eyes flicker between the black of the TV screen and the ever-growing pile of dog-eared, trampled-on, half-read books stacked in front of the already-full bookshelf, itself a cheap white cube from IKEA, draped in dead fairy lights. On the bottom row: feminist manifestos from Rebecca Solnit, Simone de Beauvoir and Judith Butler. Above them, romantic Parisian fiction by Ernest Hemmingway and F. Scott Fitzgerald. To their right, counterculture beatnik rambles from Kerouac, Ginsberg and Burroughs. Scattered throughout: Freud, Jung, Goffman and Sartre.

Books are now my escape—my passage to solitude through turning my attention outwards. I frantically buy them in bursts when I find a new topic of interest. I need to know as much as I can as quickly as possible. I need answers.

When I started writing a memoir I immediately had to know who'd written the best ones. I had so many questions opening each book. Where do they start, where do they end, how often do they flash back, how long do the flashbacks last? But even before that, I would take my finger and dot it across the top line of the page, counting how many words are in that line and repeating that number to myself. I would then go down the side and do the same counting and from those two numbers I figured out how many words were on the page. It usually ended up somewhere between 330 and 360. Sometimes 400, sometimes 280. I'd then look for spaces between paragraphs, and the section breaks, and the chapter lengths. I would breathe in, then assess the grammar: how long is a typical sentence by this author, where do their commas go, when do they use a semicolon, a colon, a dash.

There's another stack of books on the table in front of me, with Carrie Fisher at the base and Bob Dylan at the top, and a stack by my feet made up of Charles Bukowski, who wrote *Post Office* in twenty-eight days; Andre Agassi, who didn't write his own book—though his ghostwriter J.R. Moehringer says there were occasions where he was so ingrained in Agassi's mindset that he was shocked when Agassi would walk into the room and remind him that he was not his subject—and Anthony Bourdain. Of late, Bourdain has become my best friend. Death makes people more intriguing to me. Or more so, I find myself enamoured by the untapped potential that will always exist under the moniker of what could've been.

I flick open to a page of Bourdain's *Kitchen Confidential* and there he is in Los Angeles, hacking at a dead Christmas tree amid the depths of a heroin addiction. I stop reading and fold the corner of the page over. I'm wary of reading too much when I write—or sometimes reading at all. More than just counting the words per page, I tend to imitate whoever it is that I am reading; my words become theirs. Or vice versa.

Though I love books, they scare me. Other writers' words make my own seem so stale and unimportant. Didion. Sontag. Cusk. Camus. Shakespeare. King. Albertine. They strike me with their unfamiliarity, and evoke an estrangement that grips my mind.

I write in a constant struggle with authenticity, forever circling the blurred edges of my voice. This past week I've tried to be an emotionally stunted Uber driver who falls in love with a passenger; tried to witness two young boys in Bonds chesty singlets punching each other in the face before embracing to dance on a jetty in their regressive steel-making mining port town; tried to embark on a road trip with a heartbroken boy and Charles Bukowski; and tried to live the life of a teenage sex worker named Marla who hoards the secrets of the lonely men of her town and dreams of escaping. In each character are parts of myself. And soon enough they fall over because I don't know what they should do, where they should go, what they should say or how they should end up.

On a plastic rack behind me rests four guitars. A knock-off Cherry Sunburst Gibson Hummingbird Vintage that hasn't been touched since an unsuccessful recording trip to Vincentia; a shitty thirty-dollar second-hand nylon-string acoustic purchased from an Albanian backpacker which I have to tune after every song; a metallic-green Stratocaster with a still-broken high E from the night I threw it on to the ground on the main stage at Oxford Art Factory in Darlinghurst; and a Fender Telecaster with a cigarette-tray bridge—formerly owned by an Australian jazz icon whose name I forget—that I have only played a handful of times.

When you pick up a new guitar, thoughts and melodies you didn't know were there in your head are pulled from obscurity. Noel Gallagher wrote 'Live Forever' on a 1960s Gibson Les Paul, formerly owned by Pete Townshend, lent to him by Johnny Marr. Noel thinks that guitars have *souls*. Whatever you want to call it, when I get my hands on a guitar I try not to let go of it for a few days in order to suck that enchantment completely dry. The fretboard in your hand, the strings against your calloused fingers, the way its body rests against yours: it's an almost opiatic feeling. But too soon that feeling fades, the creative wheels stop turning—you can force it, you can still produce, but the songs start sounding the same, which is why I usually sell old guitars so I can buy their replacement. A Fender Thinline Telecaster replaced by a white Stratocaster replaced by a Kurt Cobain Fender Jaguar replaced by the Sunburst Ashtray tele I have now; it gathers dust as its deadened strings slowly detune. I imagine I will sell it soon.

There's a hard drive somewhere here containing the two hundred odd songs I have written and recorded. When I write a song I have to finish writing it the same day because I'm scared that I'll lose the spark, or that I'll allow myself to think endlessly about where it could go and it'll lose its essence. You can tell which music I'm really into listening to at any given point by the music I'm making. I steal production, I steal sounds, I steal textures. Neal and Nadia, the heads of my record label, usually pick it straight away.

I haven't felt like making music in months, though I've agreed to play a set this Friday. The last three gigs I've played have been with completely different line-ups, and completely different song lists, and all the time I'm up there hoping that something will finally click and feel right and the room will be filled with people who soon will say, 'I was there that first set.' This time, however, I think I'm going to go it alone—just me and a guitar on stage. I'm nervous, but I tell myself that it's *okay* because even if I don't enjoy it, I'll still find myself back here in my room playing guitar where only I can hear, and that is enough for me.

Blu-tacked to the wall above my guitars is a large poster of a black-haired Uma Thurman cradling a cigarette near her cherry-red lips. She lies on top of a bed, knees bent, feet crossed in the air. Large yellow letters spell out *Pulp Fiction* and her eyes follow me around the room. On a shelf in a large white cupboard are two tabs of acid which I bought on my birthday but still haven't done. I can trace them back to my re-reading of *Fear and Loathing in Las Vegas* at the time. There's also a teenth of weed that Dom gave me, sitting in a plastic ziplock next to a pouch of JPS gold tobacco, slim yellow filters and rectangular papers. A Remington Monarch 1 typewriter sits on the table with its body smudged by fresh ribbon ink—an unsuccessful venture on my part—and dead pot plants that I keep forgetting to water rest on top of fold-ed-over bath towels. I've started using the typewriter more of late. I appreciate that it transcribes more than just the words, capturing in some way the feeling behind those words. If you type with hesitation, the letters are faint. If you write in haste, the ferocity is captured in missed spaces and overlapped letters. I welcome the honesty of it and the imperfection it doesn't seek to correct.

Underneath the lounge on which I sit is a messily coiled red Fender lead on a floral rug that once hung from the tin wall of the underground storage locker where my first band rehearsed. A bowl of congealed cornflakes—last night's dinner—sits in the sink, a microwave with nowhere to be plugged in rests on top of the fridge, and the diaries from my footballing days lie beneath the wooden panels of my bedframe.

Empty bottles of cheap Aldi wine line the windowsill in the kitchen. I don't have an expensive palate, which I tell myself is only a blessing. When Grace and I drink a glass of red we take a sip and joke to each other, 'Hmm, tastes like a red.' I buy wine mainly based off the look of the label. Anything that looks French, because even though I've never been to France I've romanticised it in my head.

The fan spins and spins and I need to get out of here. I grab my keys and the garage door slowly rises. As I walk up the road towards the café I write at most days, I can see the tops of four white cranes turning steadily in the sky as they help construct the new football stadium in Moore Park. The foundations have slowly risen from the rubble of the old.

10.4.21

We're standing in the changerooms.

I can hear my teammates' plastic studs pittering on the concrete floor as they pace around. Somebody calls out asking where we should put our water bottles. 'In the blue tub,' the response.

On Thursday night, we trained under lights that barely covered the surface of a ground housing no goal posts. The grass was unevenly mowed and the centre square was roped off because the unused cricket pitch was still the priority. We congregated by the white steel picket fence and Deano announced that I'd been voted as captain for the year. The team clapped, and I smiled, and then we did our warmup.

I look at Deano now—I'm wearing his old boots, which are starting to split at the sides. He looks back, calls me *skip* and says I can lead the boys out when I'm ready.

We file into a line and run out onto the ground. The same ground where I played my first game of Australian rules Football twelve years ago. It sits next to Greenway Oval, where I first wore the blue and white of the Pennant Hills Stags as a five-year-old boy who dreamt of being fullback for the Australian rugby league team one day.

The reserves, who have just won by a point, form a tunnel and slap our hands and call out our names as we jog onto the ground. We run half a lap of the square and then the team heads down to one end for a kick while I walk towards the middle of the ground for the coin toss.

I shake the umpires' hands and call tails. It's heads, but we still go with the breeze in the first quarter.

I walk back towards my team and pull them in tight. Gripping a jumper in each hand, I look into the eyes of my teammates.

I say that this is exciting for us all; that it's round one of a new season and that all they have to do is bring who they are to the field.

'Bring your strengths,' I say, 'that's all I ask.'

We break. I move towards the centre circle, take my position. Then wait.

A whistle blows. The ball climbs into the air.

———

After the game, I drive home through the Sydney Harbour Tunnel. Grace has never watched a game of football before and she says she enjoyed seeing me play.

'Where are you playing next week?' she asks. 'I want to come and watch again.'

I laugh to myself because with Grace, I feel I could do anything and she would be impressed. I'm the same with her.

Side stage at every show I can be, a smile on my face. Ever in awe of her ability to make any item of clothing from the Vinnies on Oxford Street look like it belongs on a fashion runway and her one-of-a-kind reverse parking method.

We get to hers, change, then go to see a movie at the Ritz. In the theatre, my phone vibrates. A text from Deano: *bloody nice having you back on the field with me.*

At home, I shower and look through the window towards the city.

I have scratches on my knees and across my chest from the game. I've got a lot of things coming up—mainly, the submission of this manuscript in two days—but you know what? I'm looking forward to playing footy again next week.

Though that's something I'll think about when Saturday comes around.

CODA

The spaced white lines on the road accelerate before disappearing into the dashboard. There are a few clouds scattered in the sky, but above is mainly blue.

Grace is driving, so the windows are down. She likes moving air when she drives.

Our fingers are interlocked and resting in her lap. Every few minutes I squeeze and wait for her to respond. She always does, squeezing back. It's nice.

She turns to look at me for a moment and I see the widow's peak on her hairline and I smile.

I remind her about the night we first met. Three years ago, at her gig. The one that I went to because Rich had suggested it; Rich who played bass in my band, a band that I formed because I met Dicko, Dicko who I met because I no longer wanted to play football.

Grace and I went on one date after that, sitting in a café and talking about Amy Winehouse and music. Then we didn't talk for two-and-a-half years.

'It's funny,' she says, 'how that happened, and now I'm in love with you.'

'I guess I just wasn't ready at the time.'

As we drive through the valley I fix my eyes on a white weatherboard house a few hundred metres away. A line of tall pine trees runs beside it, and timber posts connected by steel wire mark the property lines. I think to myself what it would've been like to grow up surrounded by the walls of that house. Who would I be? Where would I be?

Richard Ashcroft sings through the car radio, and I put my fingers in my mouth.

ACKNOWLEDGEMENTS

To Jane for believing in an untested writer.

To Sam for seeing the trunk of the tree through the weeds.

To Tessa for getting me across the line.

To Keeva for the art of the story.

To Neal and Nadz for seeing that the pieces will come together one day.

To the baristas who remembered my order and let me write after closing hours.

To Kurt Cobain, Noel Gallagher and Joan Didion for many reasons.

To Horse, the Sydney Swans staff, and all of my coaches for your time, energy, effort and care.

To Deano for helping me find my way back. Sorry about the chairs still.

To Kieren and Charlotte for patience and family.

To Dom and the Mixed Business for inspiration and support.

To Lloyd for time spent watching buses.

To Shawry for more than football.

To Tina, Hamish and Lily for acceptance.
To Grace, for being three steps to the left—
    and for simply being Grace.

And to football.
For whatever our relationship may be, we are here now.
And through it all, some joys shine clear.